NAUGHTY PARIS
A Lady's Guide to the Sexy City

NAUGHTY PARIS

A Lady's Guide to the Sexy City

HEATHER STIMMLER-HALL

NAUGHTY PARIS
A LADY'S GUIDE TO THE SEXY CITY

Text copyright © 2008 Heather Stimmler-Hall
Photos copyright © 2008 Loop Photography (except where noted)

First Edition, 2008

ISBN 978-2-9531870-0-7

Published in France by Fleur-de-Lire Press
77 avenue des Gobelins, 75013 Paris
www.naughtyparisguide.com

Designed by *the*BookDesigners, San Francisco, CA | *www.bookdesigners.com*
Printed and bound in China through *the*BookDesigners

CAVEAT EMPTOR

As much as we like to think we were exhaustive in our research, places close, times change, obnoxious lowlifes get admitted into our favorite clubs and the Artful Dodger strikes just when you've purchased that darling new clutch purse. The author and publisher of Naughty Paris cannot accept responsibility for facts that become outdated, wardrobe failure, or for any inadvertent errors or omissions in this guide. Confirm in advance when it matters.

Dépôt légal: juillet 2008
Imprimé en Chine

CONTENTS

PART I

Bienvenue à Paris

AN INVITATION TO
NAUGHTY PARIS

"Paris is a place where women are truly liberated"

Paris is arguably the sexiest city in the world. As home to the historic Moulin Rouge, inspiration for Henry Miller's scandalous novels, and the setting for the series finale of *Sex and the City*, the French capital has become the mythical embodiment of all that is romantic, passionate, decadent, and hedonistic. It's not just about sex, *Mesdames*. The pursuit of pleasure permeates every aspect of Parisian culture, so that even the cuisine, the fashion and the language are elevated to sensual experiences. It's no wonder so many women are drawn to the City of Light. Its unspoken promise of sexual (re) discovery speaks to our feminine sensibilities and inspires us to embrace our hidden desires. Paris, we feel intuitively, is a place where women are truly liberated.

Yet aside from the heavily promoted cabaret shows, the city's truly naughty side has remained an elusive fantasy for most visitors. Until now. Naughty Paris is your personal invitation to discover the sexy side of the city you always knew existed, from swingers clubs and striptease classes to fetish parties and erotic art tours. But this guide is not just about breaking taboos, it's also about capturing the right mood to incite – not extinguish – your passion. A careful selection of intimate and stylish hotels, bars, restaurants and dance clubs will help you set the scene for seduction, while the sexy lingerie boutiques, pampering spas and naughty toy shops will help awaken your inner *femme fatale*.

One becomes aware in France, after having lived in America, that sex pervades the air. It's there all around you, like a fluid.

—HENRY MILLER

Naughty...but Nice

Naughty Paris is first and foremost a lady's guide. It reveals a sexy and provocative city seen through the eyes of the fairer sex, for women who are no longer girls but who still want to have fun. On our own terms, of course. You won't find anything nasty, seedy, illegal or disrespectful between these sheets. A lady's guide has no place for brothels, escorts, peep shows or lap dancing clubs. This is not a manual for getting lucky, nor is it the last word on sex in this city. If you're already well-initiated in the libertine "lifestyle" you may find Naughty Paris charmingly tame. If you're the kind of woman who blushes in the lingerie department, then you might find it positively shocking. Whether innocently intrigued or downright daring, only you can decide which naughty pleasures are for you. This guide is simply a menu of the many sensual delights Paris has to offer to discerning ladies, not a prescription for wanton debauchery that you must follow or risk feeling like a prude. Whether you want to be titillated by a saucy cabaret or seduced in the city's most exclusive sex clubs, this guide provides you with all the information you need to choose your own naughty adventure.

Naughty Paris is *not* for Everyone

To fully enjoy the establishments and opportunities that this guide presents, you should be a lady of legal age. In France that age is 18, and it applies to alcohol consumption as well as adults-only clubs. You should also be of sound mind and body, have a strong sense of self, of dignity, of direction (no maps here!) and – most importantly – of humor. With your tongue firmly in cheek when needed, your mind opened, and your preconceived notions and judgments aside, get ready to have some fun!

ENJOY NAUGHTY PARIS

Be the sex goddess you always knew you were.

On Your Own

The exhilarating freedom, the endless possibilities, the lingering glances from handsome locals... Paris is a whole new city for women traveling solo. People are friendlier, more helpful, and more likely to strike up a conversation than if you were traveling with friends or a partner. Enjoy the rewards of your independence. Spoil yourself with a day of self-pampering, shopping for shoes, or reading Anaïs Nin's naughty diaries on a sunny café terrace. This guide includes a special selection of hotels suitable for independent women, as well bars and restaurants "For the Ladies" that are all solo-female-friendly.

With the Ladies

Nothing brings out a woman's sexiness more than the laughter and joy we experience with our closest friends. An excellent destination for bachelorettes, best friends, or elegant empty-nesters rediscovering the joys of feminine company, Paris never fails to inspire female bonding excursions. Whether it's a visit to the city's racy female-friendly toy boutiques, ladies night cocktails in the swankiest locals' bars, or a naughty male striptease show and pole-dancing lesson, some things are just more fun with friends. And when things get wild, you know you can all agree on one thing: "What happens in Paris, stays in Paris."

With Him

He may be your husband of 20 years or the charming young Frenchman who was wooing you all night at the bar. That's your business. This guide will help you live out your fantasies, whether you're here to inject a bit of Parisian naughtiness into a long term relationship or to engage in a steamy tryst. Check into a sexy boutique hotel, feed each other oysters in a candlelit restaurant, and flirt shamelessly in a secluded corner of an intimate bar. And if the mood is right and your accomplice willing, Naughty Paris can open the doors to the city's most exclusive libertine clubs and fetish soirées. With this guide, you can be the sex goddess you always knew you were.

Parlez-Vous Français?

You don't have to be a cunning linguist to interact with the Parisians. In the rare cases where no English is understood at all, your body language, a few essential French words and a patient attitude are all you need to ease open the gates of communication.

A NAUGHTY

PARISIAN HISTORY PRIMER

> *The French reveled in flaunting their liberal beliefs and hedonistic activities.*

If Parisians seem more sexually sophisticated than their Anglo-Saxon counterparts, it's only because they've had a long time to perfect their naughty ways. Paris is a city where the quest for *joie de vivre* has long been taken to its debauched extremes, with a reputation as a capital of forbidden pleasures and illicit indulgences spanning centuries. From royal dalliances of Reine Margot in the 16th century to the high-class brothels of the early 20th century, even today we remain enchanted and fascinated by the tales of those who once made Paris their playground for erotic exploits.

The Age of (Sexual) Enlightenment

Naughtiness is as old as the city itself, but it wasn't until the social and moral upheavals of the 18th century that Parisians began openly practicing what was once carefully hidden behind locked doors. Inspired by the Enlightenment ideals of atheism and antiroyalism, the pre-Revolutionary intellectuals known as *libertins* denounced religious conventions such as chastity and monogamy. As opposition to the Church and King continued to grow, support for legalized prostitution and liberal sexual practices spread through the city's fashionable circles. A whole new code of seduction – manipulative, self-serving, and heartless – was defined by Choderlos de Laclos' influential novel *Les Liaisons Dangereuses*. "Pleasure at any price" (*Plaisir a tout prix*) became a common motto among the nobility, taken to its sadistic extremes by the infamous Marquis de Sade, who spent thirty years of his life imprisoned for his pornographic writings and sexually violent perversions.

Paris, like every pretty woman, is subject to inexplicable whims of beauty and ugliness.

— *HONORE DE BALZAC*

The Sexual Revolution

When the city's politics spiraled out of control during the 1789 Revolution and the subsequent Terror, sexual liberty became as much a part of the innate Rights of Man as *liberté*, *egalité*, or *fraternité*. Prostitution and pornography flourished, and nightly erotic 'shows' were conducted in such public areas as the Palais-Royal and the Place Dauphine. Women could be found for the willing in one of the many burgeoning brothels or cruising the streets near a *hotel de passe* that rented rooms by the hour. Though the same vices could be found in cities around the world, Paris began to set itself apart from other European capitals with its unabashed view of sexuality. Unhampered by secrecy, the French reveled – and still do, to a certain extent – in flaunting their liberal beliefs and hedonistic activities as evidence of their lack of Puritanical prudery.

Parisian Brothels

After the chaos of the Revolution, the Empire imposed its own sense of order on the new sexual mores of the city in the 19th century. More than 180 of the infamous *maisons de tolerance*, brothels legally registered by the State, were operating in Paris by 1810. Strictly regulated by French law, each employee was registered and weekly health-inspections were mandatory. Most brothels were found in the artistic enclaves of Montmartre and Montparnasse, offering customers the realization of their wildest fantasies — for the right price. Costumes, theatre sets, and a plethora of women and boys were kept at hand to reenact any flight of fancy. Their opulent settings and cabaret entertainment attracted some of the most illustrious figures of the early 20th century, such as Humphrey Bogart, Mae West, Edith Piaf and even the Prince of Wales (future King Edward VII), who supposedly bathed in a copper tub filled with Champagne at Le Chabanais.

Cabarets and Cancans

The French cabaret scene emerged alongside the brothels at the end of the 19th century, particularly in Montmartre's red-light district of Pigalle. This colorful and raunchy world, immortalized in the paintings of Henri de Toulouse-Lautrec, allowed men and women of all classes to escape the usual rules and social barriers. The brothel girls who made up the original dancers at the famous Moulin Rouge, opened in 1889, performed a vulgar and provocative interpretation of the traditional working-class party dance known as the Cancan. Audiences were both shocked and enthralled. In a Parisian nightlife guide published in 1898, the French Cancan dancers are described as "an army of young girls who dance this divine hullabaloo...with such elasticity when they launch their legs upwards that we may presume that they are at least as flexible with their morals." As the popularity of dance hall entertainment grew, the "working girls" were replaced by the professional dancers who continue to impress us today with synchronized high kicks, rather than sexual high jinks.

You can find women who have never had an affair, but it is hard to find a woman who has had just one.

– 17TH-CENTURY WRITER,
DUC DE LA ROCHEFOUCAULD

19th-century Courtesans

Somewhere between the low-brow world of brothels and the respectable world of the *haute monde*, were the pampered ladies of the *demimonde*. Also known as *les Grandes Horizontales*, these courtesans became a mainstay of high society, always in the public eye despite their notoriety and questionable morals. The era's best-known *demimondaines* were Marie Duplessis, La Présidente, La Païva and Cora Pearl, veritable celebrities who were wooed publicly by men such as Charles Baudelaire and Prince Napoléon. Neither prostitutes nor mistresses, they lived extravagantly on the favors of their rich lovers and enjoyed a level of freedom from the strict social codes that upper class women were expected to follow.

The Crazy Years

After the hardships of the Great War, Paris rebounded with another wave of joyous hedonism known as *Les Années Folles*. An influx of pleasure-seeking Americans, fleeing Prohibition and close-mindedness back home, arrived just in time to take advantage of the *laissez-faire* party atmosphere and the dollar's strong exchange rate. The prominence of eroticism and liberal sexuality inspired the works of writers and artists such as Henry Miller, Anaïs Nin, Man Ray, Brassaï, and the Surrealist intellectual Andre Breton, who viewed sex as the most important of man's irrational urges. Famous lesbians like Gertrude Stein and the wild child Natalie Barney lived their lifestyle openly, hosting influential *salons* in their Montparnasse homes, while the young African-American dancer Josephine Baker became an overnight sex symbol when her 1925 Revue Nègre debuted at the Théâtre des Champs-Elysées. The emergence during this period of the first "Made in Paris" pornographic films and electronic vibrators finally sealed the city's reputation as the European capital of naughtiness. Black Tuesday brought an end to the free-flowing Champagne in 1929, but the spirit of the times lived on in novels such as Henry Miller's *Tropic of Cancer*. "At last," said poet Ezra Pound, "an unprintable book that is fit to read."

The Rise & Fall

The popularity of Paris as a destination for carnal diversions gave rise to a whole new industry of travel guides catering to male visitors. In Bruce Reynolds' 1927 guidebook, *Paris with the Lid Lifted*, American and English travelers were walked through such delicate social interactions as picking up a Parisian woman or finding and utilizing the services of the neighborhood brothel. As other industries (and countries) crumbled during the World Wars, the Parisian sex industry continued to thrive during the Occupation with brothels that catered specifically to Officers or other Ranks, as well as to their usual clients. Arletty, an ex-prostitute and later star of *Les Enfants du Paradise*, summed it up: "My heart is French, but my ass belongs to the world." But after the Liberation, this lax attitude toward enemy relations was just another reason to close down the brothels for good. In 1946 French authorities — acting on the orders of Marthe Richard, an influential World War I spy and ex-prostitute — shut down the *maisons de tolerance* and auctioned off their glitzy interiors. Far from putting an end to the sexual activities of Parisians and visitors, however, these closures merely pushed traditional prostitution underground, while opening avenues for new expressions of eroticism.

> *It's true that the French have a certain obsession with sex, but it's a particularly adult obsession. France is the thriftiest of all nations; to a Frenchman sex provides the most economical way to have fun. The French are a logical race.*
>
> — HOLLYWOOD SCREENWRITER *ANITA LOOS*

Cultural Revolution

Undeterred by Marthe Richard and her name-bearing law, Paris kept her place in lascivious circles with her leading role in the cultural revolutions that would eventually loosen the binds of a very conservative post-war France. Existentialist writer Simone de Beauvoir gained fame in 1949 for her feminist treatise *The Second* Sex, as well as for her "untraditional" lifelong relationship with Jean-Paul Sartre. In the 1950s, the original Paris-based Olympia Press published erotic and controversial novels including Nabokov's *Lolita*, J. P. Donleavy's *Ginger Man*, and Pauline Réage's *Story of O*, and American beat poet and gay rights activist Allen Ginsberg set up residence — and a following — on the Left Bank.

But the French were uncharacteristically behind their Anglophone contemporaries on one front, only approving the sale of the birth control pill in 1967. Students at the University of Paris, protesting their institutionalized "sexual repression" symbolized by the separate academic buildings for men and women, sparked nationwide general strikes in May 1968 that would eventually usher in a new era of free love and liberal thinking. Sexual liberation was so much at the forefront of the French social culture of the time that film censorship was almost entirely removed in 1973. A year later the controversial soft porn film *Emmanuelle* (based on the 1957 novel by Emmanuelle Arsan) became an overnight success, with more than 50 million spectators around the world, a dozen spin-offs, and a decade-long run at a Champs-Elysées movie theatre. Eroticism had once again trumped its more priggish relations, and libertinism, exhibitionism, and fetishes became part of the everyday sexual landscape.

Modern Naughtiness

Today, many of promiscuous Paris' landmarks bear little resemblance to their past selves, and visitors seeking the sublime often find that the erotic has long since given way to the hardcore. Pigalle is overrun with peep shows, "hostess" bars, and their pushy sidewalk hustlers preying on unsuspecting male passers-by. And since the intervention of Marthe Richard, Parisian brothels and prostitution along the Rue St-Denis have been almost wholly appropriated by street pimps and impoverished immigrants. On the flip side, sexuality is such a commonplace and commercialized aspect of the modern cityscape that it's become almost banal. Sex-saturated images are everywhere in French advertising, the Moulin Rouge allows children to attend its cabaret show, and even the Paris Tourism office now promotes lap dancing clubs on its website.

For Us, By Us

Not surprisingly, women have been at the forefront of the city's latest naughty rebirth. Female-owned swinger's clubs and boudoir-like sex toy shops bring a lady's touch to what was once a very masculine domain, the art of burlesque strip-tease has made a comeback, and no other book caused more of a sensation than the nymphomanic memoirs of Catherine Millet (*Catherine M*), a respected art critic and founder of the high-brow art magazine, *Art Press*. One of the most controversial and daring film directors of the moment is Catherine Breillat, whose highly intellectual erotic films mixed genres when she cast porn star Rocco Siffredi in her 1999 film *Romance*. It seems only fitting that the absolutely fabulous Pamela Harriman would become ambassador to France under President Clinton. Respectfully called "The greatest courtesan of the century" by legendary broadcaster Bill Paley for her many illustrious marriages and lovers, she was the first female foreign diplomat awarded France's Grand Cross of the Legion of Honor. The French still appreciate a lady who knows how to have fun.

No Burning in Hell

During the politically turbulent 1800s, government censorship tried to reign in the unfettered sexuality of the preceding century. Any printed materials deemed "contrary to good morals" were confiscated and banned. But not burned. A special collection, kept in a locked cabinet of the Bibliothèque Nationale (National Library) was created in the 1830s by state librarians who had the foresight to collect everything that could be of cultural or historic interest to future scholars, including banned books, erotic prints and pornographic pamphlets. Known officially as L'Enfer, its 1700-strong collection was originally made up of salacious books from the Royal Library, then supplemented throughout the century by private collections confiscated during raids and customs inspections, particularly under the Second Empire. Only bona fide scholars who could prove the necessity of seeing particular works were permitted access to the collection, which only reinforced its mythical reputation. Evolving public morals oblige, L'Enfer was symbolically closed in 1969 (although the collection was reassembled in 1983 for practical purposes). Yet it wasn't until 2007 that 350 representative works were finally presented to the general public (over the age of 16) in the National Library exposition "L'Enfer de la Bibliothèque: Eros au Secret."

Five Books to Feed Your Mind

Don't know the Belle Epoch from the Lost Generation? Confused by references to
St-Germain or Montmartre? Sometimes a little historical context is in order.
Go from clueless to clever with a little help from these books.

We'll always have Paris: Sex & Love in the City of Light (by John Baxter)
The personal journey of an American writer that cleverly intertwines sex (with a history
of Parisian brothels and swinger's scene) and love (his move to Paris to start a family
with a French woman).

Paris Was a Woman: Portraits from the Left Bank (by Andrea Weiss)
Also a documentary film, this inspirational book recounts the amazing lives of women who left their home countries to come to Paris between the wars for the freedom to be artists, poets, independent book sellers, and, yes, even lovers.

Kiki's Paris: Artists and Lovers 1900-1930 (by Billy Kluver and Julie Martin)
An intimate biography of Alice Prin, aka Kiki de Montparnasse, an outrageous, charming and beautiful artist's model – and often lover – to some of the greatest figures of the Parisian art world: Man Ray, Picasso, Brancusi, Matisse, Modigliani, Cocteau…

Into a Paris Quartier (by Diane Johnson)
The author of "Le Divorce" writes an engaging portrait of St-Germain-des-Prés, its history, haunts and legendary residents, including Queen Margot, Thomas Jefferson, Josephine Bonaparte, Gertrude Stein, Oscar Wilde, and D'Artagnan.

The Essence of Style: How the French Invented High Fashion, Fine Food, Chic Cafes, Style, Sophistication, and Glamour (by Joan DeJean)
Of course you already *knew* that the French are synonymous with style, but did you know they *invented* it? A fascinating study of how the Sun King Louis XIV forever changed our perception of luxury and fine living.

ON FRENCH MEN

The Parisian metrosexual is a lean, mean seduction machine. And he knows it.

French men, according to any number of surveys, magazine articles and talk shows, are considered the best lovers in the world. While it would be presumptuous to assign sexual superiority to any particular nationality, stereotypes exist because they often contain a grain of truth. The French certainly have a flair for romance, but they are also complicated creatures full of contradictions. French men can be both imperious and wildly passionate, keenly sensitive and carelessly cruel. And for every over-confident Don Juan there's a tongue-tied Frenchmen too timid to approach a beautiful woman. French men, especially Parisians are different from American men, from British men…probably from all other men! This is not meant to be the last word on *les français*, but it should help give you an idea of what to expect should you have the opportunity to meet them during your Parisian sojourn.

The Frenchman, by nature, is sensuous and sensitive. He has intelligence, which makes him tired of life sooner than other kinds of men. He is not athletic: he sees the futility of the pursuit of fame; the climate at times depresses him...

—ANAÏS NIN

Natural Born Romantics

French men don't choose to be more romantic; they're just born that way, blessed with Latin genes and a history of courtly love dating back to the Medieval troubadours. Immersed in a culture that lovingly savors cuisine, wine, art and beauty, Parisian men simply can't help but know a thing or two about vintage Champagne, fine-tailored shirts, 18th-century art, or how to host a memorable dinner party without breaking a sweat. When a French man invites you for a picnic of wine and cheese on the quays of the Seine followed by an art house film screening in the Latin Quarter, he's not putting on an act to impress you. That's just the way of life for the average Parisian. Not that they aren't aware of the way their seductive culture — especially the French language — makes foreign women swoon. He may act blasé about the Eiffel Tower, but if your Frenchman prefers to stroll back from the restaurant along the banks of the Seine rather than taking a taxi, it's because he's keenly aware of the mood-enhancing effects of the Parisian skyline.

"The French way of hitting on a girl is definitely more romantic," observes Veronica, an American journalist who has lived in France for close to a decade. "They appeal to what women are looking for."

Metrosexual Tendencies

Many heterosexual Parisian men have adopted the metrosexual lifestyle, shamelessly meticulous about their physical appearance in a way that used to be reserved for boys who like boys. Like modern dandies, they prefer Italian leather shoes to sneakers, designer jeans and fitted jackets rather than sweatshirts. They have as many beauty products in their bathroom as we ladies do. And while these Parisian men may sport sexy stubble, they are not afraid of hair removal below the belt. But don't believe for one moment that all of this preening makes them effeminate. The Parisian metrosexual is a lean, mean seduction machine. And he knows it. Still, a touch of arrogance is easy to forgive in any gentleman considerate enough to keep his family jewels clean shaven.

The Art of Flirtation

You have to be very fond of men. Very, very fond. You have to be very fond of them to love them. Otherwise they're simply unbearable.

—MARGUERITE DURAS

On the street, in cafés, at the market, or even in the office... the French do it everywhere. No location is too banal nor any occasion too serious for a bit of harmless flirting. And the best part is that everyone can participate in this equal-opportunity pastime, no matter what your age or marital status. First-time visitors may initially be shocked by the knowing winks and appreciative compliments that they receive throughout their stay, especially when they come from men who are obviously not single, or when there's a significant age difference... in either direction. While eye contact and a smile in a nightclub will be taken as an open invitation to make a pass, in most situations flirting is merely a pleasant form of communication. French women bask in flirtatious attention from shopkeepers and waiters; even if there's no real intention (or interest) in going further, it puts a smile on everyone's face.

After several years on the French dating scene before marrying her own Parisian, American-born editor Allison Lightwine knows a thing or two about the local seduction techniques. "When it comes to chatting up women, the world is a Frenchman's oyster. While flirting is a fact of life in French culture, it's not necessarily used as means to get a girl into the *boudoir*. Both men and women regard flirting as a dance of seduction that spices up the daily grind. If it leads to something more, *pourquoi pas?*"

"In Paris, where desire is considered natural rather than sinful, anything can take place…if you want it to," adds Amy, a Canadian-born poet and longtime Paris resident.

A Stereotypical Catch-22

French men aren't the only ones suffering from unfair stereotyping. Some men in Paris, French and otherwise, seem to consider foreign women as easy sexual conquests. It doesn't help that they tend to form their opinions based on certain aspects of American and British pop culture like "Sex & the City," Paris Hilton, "Bridget Jones' Diary," and wet t-shirt contests. On the flip side, Americans in particular also get labeled as Puritanical prudes thanks to our country's seemingly collective outrage over Janet Jackson's wardrobe failure, Monica Lewinsky, and the lack of paper gowns in French doctors' offices. Damned if you do, damned if you don't? Of course, it would be silly to try to divine the intentions of your Parisian suitors, so just be yourself and don't feel single-handedly responsible for rehabilitating your country's reputation.

The flamboyant blonde Brit Rebecca Catt fondly recalls her party days as a young and very single fashion editor in Paris. "Being blonde and buxom is a sure-fire route for a head-on collision with half the city. Blonde = Scandinavian = sex addict. And wearing colorful clothes and not the national uniform of black also lays you seriously open to attack. Random men would come up to me in the street and invite me for coffee with salacious looks in their eyes, while their female counterparts would almost push me off the pavement with their eyes shooting out spiky arrows of disapproval."

French Men Try Harder

Whether it's typical Gallic arrogance, the thrill of the chase, or the expectations of the demanding *Parisiennes*, very little can deter an amorous Frenchman once he's in hot pursuit. In America, "No means No." In France, no means "I'm not convinced." Don't be surprised if his powers of persuasion may eventually win you over. If not, be prepared to stand your ground. A lady never gives into pressure just to be "polite." If he persists, send him your iciest glare or walk away, but don't explain yourself or let him engage you in a debate. Verbal sparring for a Frenchman is almost as much fun as sex, even if he has to do it in broken English. Silence is the best tactic.

"I remember the general manager of a huge company, a real French man," recounts Nicolas, a French businessman in his 40s. "He had a meeting to negotiate a very complex dismissal with an employee and his lawyer, yet he spent the whole meeting trying to seduce the lawyer. No need to tell the results!"

Dangerous Liaisons

Don't assume your suitor is single. He won't assume you are — or care either way. For the Parisian playboy, any unaccompanied (and sometimes even accompanied) woman is fair game for a *petite aventure*. "Sorry, I'm married," will not faze him in the least (see above for the reasons why). While the French haven't cornered the market in infidelity, the culture tends to romanticize the practice with a "don't ask, don't tell" policy adopted by men and women alike. This is best illustrated by the widespread tolerance of the *le cinq-à-sept* ("five to seven"), that special time of day between leaving work and arriving at home when lovers meet to engage in a bit of covert extra-curricular activity.

"The natural solution to avoiding the bad apples is to pick one that already has a stamp of approval from someone else," says Allison. "Apparently it's much more interesting to conquer occupied territory than to strike out for virgin shores!"

Rules? What Rules?

Dating etiquette is confusing enough, even without the language and cultural barriers. The French don't have any book of "Rules" to follow, but to avoid any needless embarrassment or discomfort, there are a few subtle "codes" you should know before your *rendez-vous*. If you invite him up to your hotel room for a drink, or accept to dine at his place (without any other guests), you've pretty much given him the green light for some naughty action. Of course a lady is always free to change her mind, but he would be understandably perplexed and annoyed that you sent him mixed signals. To maintain the option of a more elegant retreat, meet at a restaurant instead, or even just for drinks before deciding if you want to sit through an entire meal. It's also important to know that if a French man invites you out, he pays. This doesn't imply you're obliged to "do" anything in return. Your scintillating company is compensation enough.

"There are no rules actually, but codes… or signals," explains Nicolas. "The target is quite simple: to go or not to go together… to bed! A dinner at home is a clear signal, so there's no doubt on the issue if you accept. Assuming this mandatory part has been achieved, then we can talk for hours and enjoy the meal, where maybe the US practice is to talk for hours with no insurance of going to bed. What a big loss of time and efficiency," he adds, laughing.

Sexual Taboos

After centuries of breaking any and all sexual taboos in the pursuit of *liberté*, very little can shock or offend Parisians in the bedroom. Practices that might elicit nervous giggles back home hardly raise eyebrows in French society, where swingers' clubs and threesomes (even with two men and one woman) are practically considered mainstream. It may be prudent to know that *sex à la derrière* (not the official French term, *ahem*) is considered part of their regular sexual repertoire, not something that needs to be negotiated or discussed in advance. With the inherent language barriers and the French male tendency to act first and apologize later, you may find yourself at the receiving end of an unauthorized rear entry.

"If you go with your gut instinct and let your hair down, you might just find yourself in something like a scene out of a naughty French film – what more titillation could a girl want?" says Allison. "As long as you're ready for a no-strings-attached roll in the hay, going out with a pick-up *artiste* can be fun and sexually enlightening. Just don't expect him to call you in the morning."

People always like things that seem exotic.

—BRITISH ACTRESS/ SINGER *JANE BIRKIN*.

The Bad and the Ugly

At their worst, French men can be selfish, egotistical and blatantly manipulative in their relationships. Spoiled by their mothers (Latin roots *oblige*), they grow up thinking that every woman finds them attractive and charming. Inferiority complexes are masked by arrogance and cynicism, while their flawed Cartesian logic and distaste for outward displays of emotion (particularly by the women they've certainly wronged) make them as coldheartedly calculating as their obvious antihero, *Dangerous Liaisons'* Vicomte de Valmont. The Frenchman may wear his passion on his sleeve, but don't talk to him about love, and certainly don't ask about "the relationship". Luckily, most visitors aren't in town long enough to see their Parisian paramours transform into these fickle Doctor Hyde's.

"When I first came to France, I was rabidly pursued by a young man working for one of my company's clients. Thinking of the possible complications, I politely brushed off all of his advances – that is, until a romantic promenade after a sales conference cracked my resolve," says Allison. "Ironically, after I had capitulated and started asking about the state of our relationship, he cooled off. 'American girls are too complicated!' he groaned. Looking back, I see that he had a point. Why waste all that breath analyzing the situation when you could be making out?"

The Good News

If you've got your heart set on your very own French lover, don't bother trying to channel your inner Parisienne. Your accent when you speak the language, the way you muddle up verb conjugations and masculine and feminine nouns, or the fact that you may speak no French at all is, to many French men, sexy. Your very foreign-ness is what is most attractive.

"It's more interesting to date women who aren't from here, they're much more *exotique*," declares Alexandre, a handsome Parisian *dragueur* (flirt) at Régine's Club.
"French women can be so *difficile*," adds his friend Cyril. "We love foreign women!"

"Apparently my accent when I spoke French—which believe me I tried my darnedest to gallicise as much as possible—was sexy," says Rebecca, in her distinctly British accent. "A brief diatribe of bubbly nothings peppered with atrocious grammar was all it took to have a veritable line of suitors vying for my attention. That and of course my facility to have a good time. French girls, for all their subtle beauty, are not very good at letting their hair down. They won't leap on a table and sing "Hey big spender!" and down three tequila shots at the bar. And there you have it, my fellow Anglophones, the key utensil in our seduction tool box: Spontaneity! It's just not done over here and when administered in carefully measured doses it will win over the hearts and minds of any French *monsieur* you fancy bedding."

CyberSexy

Here are a few free websites where you can meet the locals from the comfort of your own computer. They're all in French, but you'll have no trouble finding a few who can converse in English.

www.meetic.fr (A classic dating site.)
www.easyflirt.com (A dating site divided into three categories: Love, Sex, and Gay)
www.pointscommuns.com (A site where you meet based on cultural interest such as movies, music, books, etc.)

Flirting Vocabulary

For help deciphering his sweet nothings *en français*, see the French Tongue section of the Get in the Mood chapter.

A WOMAN IN PARIS

There's a sexy, confident, feminine, feisty and powerful Parisienne inside every woman.

Paris is for Women

Women have a unique relationship with Paris. The city seduces us, inspires us, and calls to us like no other place in the world. Paris has come to embody the ideal of *liberté*, where we are free to acknowledge and embrace who we really are as women. This is, after all, where Anaïs Nin embarked on her sexual awakening, where Josephine Baker aroused audiences with her famous "banana dance," and where Kiki de Montparnasse became an enchanting muse to some of the most illustrious artists of the 20th century. Even today, women come to Paris looking for something they

> *One is not born a woman,*
> *but becomes one.*
> —SIMONE DE BEAUVOIR.

can't get at home: feminine fulfillment. Here we find the permission to let our womanly qualities shine, to be appreciated and adored and revered as the beautifully complex creatures that we are. In Paris we are neither bystanders nor objects of the cityscape, but actors and protagonists; we are the *raisons d'etre*.

We can come to City of Light and bask in the city's culture, its cuisine, and the attention we receive from charming French men. But what really intrigues us are the Parisian women. They seem unfathomable exotic birds, otherworldly and indecipherable. Yet if you were lucky enough to stay in Paris long enough, you would discover that despite their fiercely individualistic nature there are a few common traits that characterize *les Parisiennes*. And even if you're not French, you can capture the same *esprit* with the right attitude.

Parisiennes are Feminine

In Paris, women are unapologetically feminine. They wear inappropriately tall high heels to work, would never be caught dead in public without makeup, and expect men to hold the door for them. But this hardly means that they're weak. In fact, for Parisian women their femininity is their strength, not a weakness that must be overcome or ignored. The battle of the sexes exists in France like any other western country, but *les Parisiennes* choose to level the playing field using weapons of mass seduction. They make the most of their feminine wiles: charm, beauty, intuition, sensitivity, and cunning. Obviously the definition of "politically correct" and "feminism" differ from what women are used to on the other side of the Atlantic.

"French feminism has few of the sharp edges it has in America. In France, it's softer, fuzzier. The French girl can be a feminist and still unequivocally love men," writes Debra Ollivier in *Entre Nous*. In Anglophone cultures, feminism tends to focus on equality of the sexes by denying their differences, to the extreme where women are considered "just like men" in more ways than one. In France, feminism is not about being aggressive, angry, or — *mon dieu!* — masculine.

"The famous French expression *vive la différence!* (hooray for the difference!) takes the sting out of the disparity between men and women by highlighting the contrasts rather than the inequalities between the sexes," writes French author Véronique Vienne in *The Art of Being a Woman*.

Intellectually speaking, French feminism has its complicated theories and ideals based on psychoanalysis and the body. And while most of the French may be more interested in theories rather than results, Parisian women tend to take a more pragmatic approach to feminism. Instead of getting herself all worked up over the way things "should be," she adapts herself to the way things are to get what she wants.

Parisiennes are Confident

One of the most captivating qualities of Parisian women is their self confidence. They wear it like a fine couture gown, perfectly fitted to their body, their age, their style. It shows in the way they carry themselves, and the way they interact with others. What makes them so confident is their keen awareness that being attractive has very little to do with superficial looks.

While Catherine Deneuve or Brigitte Bardot may represent unattainable ideals of glamour and sophistication, most French women are not classic beauties. They tend to be rather short, with unremarkable, almost mousy features. But they more than make up for it with mental prowess. Wit, confidence, and a personal sense of style will get you further in Paris than Botox and bleached teeth. In America, boys don't make passes at girls wearing glasses. In France, however, *filles à lunettes, filles à quequettes* (loosely translates as "girls who wear glasses are girls who like male appendages"). If you're a woman in the country of love, your specs are downright sexy *à la* "naughty librarian." This just

Beyond the beauty, the sex,
the titillation, the surface,
there is a human being.
And that has to emerge.

– ACTRESS *JEANNE MOREAU*

illustrates the wider mentality in France that you don't have to be a supermodel to be attractive to the opposite sex. In fact, you don't even have to be young, thin or trendy. Liberating and equalizing, every woman has the chance to make the most of what she was born with.

*See the **Sexy You!** chapter for insider Parisian tips on looking your best.*

Parisiennes are Appreciated

What's the fun in getting dressed to the nines, teetering around in your stilettos and squeezing into a little sliver of a dress, if no one ever appreciates the effort? Even if you're really dressing up for yourself, it doesn't hurt the ego at all to receive a few respectable smiles of approval from the opposite sex. And in Paris, they'll do more than just smile. Parisian women expect to be admired and appreciated for all the hard work they put into looking good. That's why all of the chairs on café terraces face the sidewalk. In a culture that embraces all forms of pleasure without hang-ups, there's no pretense that Parisians are doing anything other than checking each other out.

For foreign women who are new to the City of Light, the attention can be a bit overwhelming. The stares, double-takes, comments and *oh là là's* can take place anywhere, from cafés and bakeries to nightclubs and museums, no matter your age or how conservatively you're dressed. To some, it may seem like borderline harassment, but whether you're flattered or annoyed by the attention, handle it with grace *à la Parisienne* and simply glide past without acknowledgment or breaking your stride. You just might find an added spring in your step or the hint of a smile on your face for the rest of the day.

Men want to adore you, Ladies. Put your guard down when you come to Paris, and let them adore you.

Parisiennes Know Their History

Despite the fact that many American girls are told that their brains are valued over beauty, this message conflicts with the airbrushed images in the media, and eventually sows the seeds of doubt. Not so with Parisian women. Sure, they have the same pressure to conform to supermodel standards, but they've got an even stronger message imbedded in their subconscious: women are powerful. They know this because, from the time they are born they are surrounded by the images, the history books, the art and the legends about the strong female role models who have shaped over two millennia of French history. From St-Geneviève, who saved the city from the Huns, to the brave Joan of Arc and the feisty Queen Eleanor of Aquitaine, Parisian girls grow up learning about their kings' mistresses, and how they were often much older and sometimes even more powerful than the monarchs themselves. French literature is full of stories that illustrate the irresistible allure of the wise and witty woman of character over the pretty and shallow ones. And Parisian mothers pass this confidence along to their daughters.

Parisiennes Know Their Worth

Parisian women are so confident in their inherent worth that they are famously intolerant of being treated as anything less than goddesses by their men. They've been called demanding, controlling, calculating – and much worse – but when a Parisian woman feels disrespected, she's a force to be reckoned with. The *sang froid* she's usually known for will suddenly give way to a storm of emotions delivered with typical Latin intensity. She will be heard, and she will not be a doormat, even if it means causing a scene in public. And if the man doesn't measure up, she simply moves on, with her characteristic Cartesian logic. "If a shoe doesn't fit, you don't buy it. Your foot isn't going to change its shape, right?" writes author Debra Ollivier in *Entre Nous*. "Same goes for men. If he's not right for you, drop him. Unless you want to walk around in pain, you move on to new merchandise."

Parisiennes are Mysterious

"American women show, Parisian women suggest," said Olivier, a young French sommelier who has lived on both sides of the Atlantic. "The way they dress, the way they act around men... there's no mystery with American women." It's true that Parisian women are notoriously hard to read. They reveal very little about themselves to anyone outside their closest circle of friends. This air of mystery puts them in a position of power, while their men are helplessly left guessing.

The French often refer to a woman's *jardin secret*, the metaphorical secret garden she keeps hidden for herself. Even her husband knows not to pry into this private space. Unlike some western cultures, the French believe it's actually healthier to have secrets in a relationship. Maybe her secret garden is simply an embarrassing beauty ritual, or a weakness for vapid romantic comedies. But it could also imply a discreet bit of plastic surgery, a hidden bank account, or a lover. But in the Parisian world of relationships, this "don't ask, don't tell" policy helps maintain a certain distance that keeps the intrigue alive.

In American culture, we're not only raised to be polite, but we're also encouraged to be outgoing and brutally honest. We think the more personal things we share about ourselves, the closer we'll be to our men (and we expect the same in return). But when you come to Paris, learn to play your cards closer to your heart. That handsome French suitor is looking for seduction, not a new pal. No need to tell him your entire life history, or even your name, for that matter. And the hint of a smile is much more intriguing than a toothy grin. To return to the garden metaphor, imagine yourself as the slightly overgrown garden labyrinth that draws him in, not the perfectly trimmed formal garden he can enjoy from the window.

Unlock Your Inner Parisienne

If truth be told, women in Anglophone cultures actually go through a lot of effort to stifle our feminine side. We enthusiastically embrace the audacious, aggressive, and inherently masculine-tinged version of sexiness, while subconsciously equating femininity with being overemotional, vulnerable, or powerless. You certainly didn't grow up in this day and age as a Modern Woman by using your feminine wiles. But as the Parisian women have shown, there's something very empowering about making the best of your womanly strengths and weaknesses. Take a break from political correctness when you come to Paris, and feel free to relax and express yourself in ways you never thought you could do back home.

We travel, some of us forever, to seek other states, other lives, other souls.

—ANAÏS NIN

Ironically, being a foreigner in Paris can give women more freedom than their French counterparts. We have no family pressures or societal expectations, and the handy tactic of feigning ignorance if we break one too many codes of conduct. There's a sexy, confident, feminine, feisty and powerful *Parisienne* inside every woman. Your trip to Paris is the chance to let her blossom as you embark on your naughty adventures!

Books for Finding Your Inner Parisienne

Two Lipsticks and a Lover (sold in the U.S. under the title *All You Need to Be Impossibly French: A Witty Investigation Into the Lives, Lusts, and Little Secrets of French Women*) by Helena Frith Powell. A fun and witty investigation into what makes French women so stylish, with practical tips and insightful interviews with French fashion icons.

The Art of Being a Woman by Véronique Vienne. A French woman's advice on the sexiness of self-acceptance and experience the "joie de vivre" of our lives.

True Pleasures: A Memoir of Women in Paris by Lucinda Holdforth. A personal journey of a woman exploring Paris, looking to transform her own life through the inspiration of the city's many celebrated rule-breakers, style-setters and divas from Colette and Coco Chanel to Marie Antoinette and Pamela Harriman.

French Women for All Seasons: A Year of Secrets, Recipes, and Pleasure by Mireille Guiliano. More secrets from the author of French Women Don't Get Fat on how to enjoy the little pleasures in life.

Entre Nous: A Woman's Guide to Finding Her Inner French Girl by Debra Ollivier. A clever and entertaining book on the French woman's secrets for being stylish, with an emphasis on making the best of what you are born with.

France, A Love Story: Women Write About the French Experience, edited by Camille Cusumano. A collection of stories by two dozen women describing the country they love and why they fell under its spell.

Fatale: How French Women Do It by Edith Kunz. A peek into the mysterious ways Frenchwomen manage to appear sexy, smart and recklessly chic without even trying.

PART II

*Your Boudoir
or Mine?*

HOTELS

Nothing will bring alive – or smother – your Naughty Paris fantasies quicker than the hotel you choose. The right one – sumptuous, sultry, sexy – will immediately inspire you to test out the mattress or run a luxuriant bath. There's something about 24-hour room service, Egyptian cotton sheets, and the convenience of a valet to hail your cab that adds to the allure of a luxury hotel. But even seedy can be sexy if you're into badboys and role playing, or need a place where your wild bachelorette party won't offend anyone. But a hotel decorated like your doctor's waiting room and catering almost exclusively to noisy tour groups is not going to do much for your libido, no matter what kind of lingerie you packed. Ditto for anything overly "charming" that relies heavily on lace doilies, Provençal fabrics, or shabby-chic furnishings as a central décor theme.

There are thousands of hotels in Paris, but these carefully selected establishments are a sure bet for *les dames* looking to set the perfect scene, whether it's for seduction or indulgent self-pampering.

HÔTEL COSTES

239 RUE ST-HONORÉ, 1ST.
TEL 01 42 44 50 50. FAX 01 42 44 50 01.
Mᵒ TUILERIES OR CONCORDE.
WWW.HOTELCOSTES.COM

Elitist? Maybe. But a lady has her standards, after all, and if you wear yours unapologetically on your sleeve, than the exclusive Hôtel Costes will do nicely. It's so *snob* they don't bother with photos or descriptions on their website, so trendy that they have bouncers instead of doormen, and so adored by the international jetset that you'll have almost no chance of getting a room during Fashion Week. But think of how good you'll look in the opulent Second Empire décor of red velour, purple satin, and gilded antique furnishings (yes, more of designer Jacques Garcia's boudoir magic). Strap on your sexiest Louboutin stilettos and mingle with the glitterati in the hotel's restaurant bar. Absurdly large designer sunglasses are *de rigueur* on the Italian courtyard terrace. Terribly underdressed? You only need to stumble out the front door to find Chanel, Galliano, Cartier, Chantal Thomass. Then test out the male reaction to your naughtiest bathing suit in the hotel's low-lit swimming pool, thoughtfully equipped with an underwater sound system (the better to enjoy the famous Hôtel Costes compilations, *bien sûr*).

HOTEL PARK HYATT VENDÔME

5 RUE DE LA PAIX, 2ND.
TEL 01 58 71 12 34. FAX 01 58 71 12 35.
Mᵒ OPÉRA
WWW.PARIS.VENDOME.HYATT.COM

You are a sleek and cultured woman, modern and exquisite. And you seek the same in a hotel. Who cares that it's part of an international chain when it's located just off the swanky Place Vendôme, home to couture jewelers such as Fred, Boucheron, and Cartier (just in case you need to introduce your darling *mec* to your sparkling best friends, *ahem*). Enjoy the relative anonymity provided by such a large hotel when checking in with that totally inappropriate lover (and try not to look too smug when a glimpse of his passport reveals your scandalous age difference). Caress the dark mahogany wood furnishings, feel the bathroom's heated limestone floors under your feet, and slip between the lush linens of your king-sized bed. Here with the ladies? The low-lit bar and haut cuisine restaurant-in-the-round offer women on the prowl ample hunting grounds (prepare for your close up with a body-buffing afternoon in the hotel's Carita spa).

MURANO URBAN RESORT

13 BOULEVARD DU TEMPLE, 3RD.
TEL 01 42 71 20 00. FAX 01 42 71 21 01.
Mᵒ FILLES DU CALVAIRE
WWW.MURANORESORT.COM

As close as Paris gets to having a sense of humor, this adult playground of giggle-inducing gadgets à la Austin Powers is both fun and sexy. The elevator walls are covered in sparkly or furry fabrics, the hallways are moodily lit with ultraviolet bulbs, the doors open via fingerprint sensor, and a bedside control panel changes the color of lights in the all-white rooms (with white shag-pile rugs). Only squares would notice the lack of doors on the sleek bathrooms. Show off your backstroke in the Deluxe Suite's private counter-current swimming pool or get right down to business in the Honeymoon Suite's shagadelic round bed. Swinging solo? Don your biggest sunglasses, your shortest mini, and your most fabulous pair of gogo boots and meet your friends for some serious flirting at the hotel's hip vodka bar (see *Wine & Dine* in **After Dark Rendez-Vous**). Sunday jazz brunches are served until 5 p.m. for those trying to sleep off any nocturnal digressions.

MARAIS HOUSE

(SOMEWHERE IN THE MARAIS...3RD)
TEL: 06 16 13 39 90 OR 01 42 74 61 36.
WWW.MARAISHOUSE.COM

Why the mysterious address, you ask? Sometimes a lady desires a bit of discretion. You wouldn't want just *anyone* wandering into your Parisian *pied-à-terre*, a 16th-century townhouse filled with expensive antiques, canopy beds, and huge stone fireplaces. Choose one of the five large bedrooms to suit you and your lover, or book the whole house and invite your girly entourage for an unforgettable bachelorette getaway. Certain luxuries are non-negotiable, such as air conditioning (*oui, Madame*), and live-in staff to prepare your breakfast in the vaulted stone dining room. You're just a short stroll from the postcard-perfect boutiques, cafés and museums of the historic Marais district, without having to bear the masses outside your double-glazed windows. And since they only give the exact address to guests, there's no need to don your elaborate Hitchcock-worthy disguises when checking in.

Splurge Bonus
THE "CHAMBRE À LA FRESQUE"

AT THE HÔTEL DES SAINTS-PÈRES
65, RUE DES SAINTS-PÈRES, 6TH. TEL 01 45 44 50 00.
WWW.PARIS-HOTEL-SAINTS-PERES.COM

This 17th-century house once belonged to Louis XIV's architect, so it's no surprise that the high ceiling of this unique room features an immense fresco, recalling the splendors of Versailles. Other historical nods include the parquet wood floors and huge clawfoot bathtub, placed indulgently across from the bed. Even for a palace hotel this room would be impressive, but when found hidden away in a tiny St-Germain boutique hotel… well, that's just the kind of secret luxury we all hope to find on our travels. Book well in advance, and don't forget your silk dressing gown.

L'HÔTEL

13 RUE DES BEAUX ARTS, 6TH.
TEL 01 44 41 99 00. FAX 01 43 25 64 81.
Mª ST-GERMAIN-DES-PRÉS
WWW.L-HOTEL.COM

The Hotel? A bit presumptuous, isn't it? *Mais non.* Its seductive pedigree dates back to the 17th century, when it was part of the palatial lair of the country's scandalous divorcée, Queen Marguerite de Valois (aka Reine Margot). In the 18th century it was transformed into a Pavillion d'Amour and, finally, a hotel where the decadent hedonist Oscar Wilde lived (and died) above his means. After an initial heyday in the Swinging Sixties, this sexy little Left Bank hotel continues to seduce its many illustrious guests, from rock stars to princesses. Let your inner diva laze amongst the richly-colored satin pillows, velour divans and silk tassels of Jacques Garcia's sumptuous décor. Dare a bit of playful eye contact with other guests in the circular, candle-lit halls overlooking the central atrium. Rooms are *Mignon* and *Bijoux* (ie tiny), each uniquely decorated in lavish, over-the-top French fabrics and antiques. Unpack your little black dress and head to the romantic, low-lit bar and restaurant, popular with the local gallery crowd. Or reserve the private pool for a languorous swim under the vaulted stone arches. Sociable ladies will appreciate the proximity to St-Germain-des-Prés's top people-watching venues, Café Flore and Deux Magots.

HÔTEL VILLA D'ESTRÉES

17 RUE GÎT LE COEUR, 6TH.
M° ST-MICHEL OR ODÉON
TEL 01 55 42 71 11, FAX 01 55 42 71 00
WWW.HOTELVILLADESTREESPARIS.COM

LE SEZZ

6 AVE FREMIET, 16TH.
M° PASSY
TEL 01 56 75 26 26, FAX 01 56 75 26 16
WWW.HOTELSEZZ.COM

The beautiful young Gabrielle d'Estrées was just 16 years old when Henri IV made her his beloved mistress in 1590. Likewise dignified, yet discreet, the Villa d'Estrées can be found on the same narrow Left Bank street where the king supposedly proclaimed his eternal adoration. The 17th-century building has ten spacious rooms, two on each floor (which can be connected for more privacy), where you can reenact your own illicit trysts in a sexy setting of modern French Empire style: dark mahogany antique furnishings, bold striped carpeting, deep red or blue wall fabrics, gorgeous black Moroccan tiled baths. A *petite* erotic bookshop is conveniently located just across the street, in case you're in need of some historic inspiration.

I like men who have a future and women who have a past.
—OSCAR WILDE

Is *monsieur* allergic to pink velour and anything gilded? A real bachelor's lair, the masculine lines and rough grey stone walls à la Frank Lloyd Wright will coax even the most reluctant Romeo into a playful mood. And if he still feigns exhaustion, go ahead and run a bubble bath while he crashes on the chrome, camp-style beds – placed suggestively in the *center* of the room. Nothing on the TV will be able to tear your voyeur's eyes away from the one-way glass revealing your seemingly (shhh...) innocent strip tease as you step into one of the largest bath tubs in Paris (be sure to request *chambre* 69). With more than enough room for *deux*, you won't be soaking solo for long, darling. And yes, there are rooms with views of the glittering Eiffel Tower, but the discreet location in the posh Passy district of west Paris is far from the tacky tourist masses.

HÔTEL DU PETIT MOULIN

29/31 RUE DE POITOU 3RD.
TEL 01 42 74 10 10. FAX 01 42 74 97 10.
Mᵒ FILLES-DU-CALVAIRE.
WWW.HOTELPETITMOULINPARIS.COM

HÔTEL BOURG-TIBOURG

19 RUE BOURG-TIBOURG, 4TH.
TEL 01 42 78 47 39. FAX 01 40 29 07 00.
Mᵒ HÔTEL DE VILLE
WWW.HOTELBOURGTIBOURG.COM

There's more than one way to immerse yourself head-to-toe in Christian Lacroix. Head to the north end of the Marais, past the contemporary art galleries and cutting edge clothing boutiques. You'll feel like a fashion insider when stepping into this discreet hotel with its original 1900 *boulangerie* façade and 17ᵗʰ-century architecture. Lacroix was given *carte blanche* to personally decorate each of the 17 rooms according to his own tastes, resulting in an explosion of styles and colors that define the French designer's fashions: shag pile carpeting and clay tiles, pink pop-art walls and toile de Jouy, antique furnishings and contemporary light fixtures. Amenities are limited to the necessities to reduce sticker shock. "It's Lacroix, baby. Pay the bill and take me shopping."

Imagine a low-lit, candle-scented hideaway decked out in a richly-colored tapestry of velvet chairs, satin pillows, silk tassels, and exotic prints. You're inside the genie's lamp, on the set of *1001 Arabian Nights*, awaiting your sheik in a cozy harem of neo-Gothic and Byzantine architectural details. With no restaurant or bar, the Bourg-Tibourg almost feels like a bed and breakfast rather than a hotel. Located on a side street of the trendy Marais district, this is the smallest hotel of the Costes empire with just 31 terribly snug rooms. Book the suite if you want enough room to show off your Oriental Dance moves.

THE FIVE

3 RUE FLATTERS, 5TH
Mᵒ GOBELINS OR CENSIER-DAUBENTON
TEL 01 43 31 74 21.
WWW.THEFIVEHOTEL.COM

Every lady should have the address of at least one discreet hideaway tucked into her purse at all times. There's no chance of being spotted when stepping out of this tiny designer boutique, well-hidden on a quiet side street of the Latin Quarter. Fiber optic fairy lights illuminate beds suspended from the ceiling or canopied in satin fringe, while aromatherapy scent diffusers and over 100 cable channels on the flat-screen TVs set the mood. Understand, these pocket-sized rooms are designed for sex, not unpacking. Leave the huge suitcases behind. You wouldn't be the first client checking in with nothing more than your lip gloss and a lover.

HOTEL AMOUR

8 RUE NAVARRE, 9TH.
TEL 01 48 78 31 80.
Mᵒ PIGALLE
WWW.HOTELAMOUR.COM

Très sexe, the aptly-named Love Hotel manages to be naughty without being seedy, despite its titillating proximity to Pigalle's redlight district. Opened in 2006, it's become prime territory for slumming Parisian hipsters — you'll see them striking their world-weary poses in the hotel's retro brasserie/bar — attracted by the porno-chic mix of avant-garde art and bargain basement prices. You, too, will refrain from looking impressed, or – *mon dieu!* – giggling at the vintage girly mags papering the walls. At least until you reach the privacy of your own room. All 20 of them are decorated with a completely different theme, most with suggestive connotations. Do you see yourself with a backdrop of black lacquered or artfully graffiti'd walls? Does a clawfoot tub squatting in the center of one room play into your fantasies? What about an exhibitionist shower in a bathroom separated by one-way bronzed glass? No robes, no TVs, no bellhops, and no Bibles to save your soul. But do enjoy the exclusive Kiehl's toiletries. Bring that bad boy who makes you feel like a porn star. Or book the party room for you and your girl friends, with a pre-stocked wet bar and large balcony overlooking the hotel's garden courtyard, perfect for fair weather stud-spotting.

Budget Bonus
HÔTEL ELDORADO

18 RUE DES DAMES, 17TH.
M° PLACE DE CLICHY
TEL 01 45 22 35 21. FAX 01 43 87 25 97.
WWW.ELDORADOHOTEL.FR

Indulge your Bohemian sensibilities at this trendy budget dive in the edgy Batignolles district.
Book one of the no-frills, flea-market chic rooms overlooking the leafy inner courtyard, shared with the neighboring wine bar "Le Bistro des Dames." Here you can mingle and flirt with up-and-coming fashion designers, artists and musicians over a glass of Côtes du Rhône. Amenities are non-existent and the location is hardly central, but at these prices you can afford to hire your own car and driver!

Afternoon Delight:
A word about "Day Use"

On the official Paris Tourism Office website, Day Use has the following description: "If you are just passing through Paris or in transit between two international flights, hotels can let rooms just for the daytime." And there might actually be some people out there who use it this way. But don't think for a second that you're the first to think of checking into a hotel for a few hours of naughty bliss. Best of all, the discounted rate means that you can test out the palatial boudoirs normally outside your budget.

How it works: Call (or just show up) and ask if there any rooms available for "Day Use" (the English term is understood). This is a very common request (and the French service industry is discreet, if anything else), so don't bother making up some silly story about why you need it only a few hours or why you have no luggage. A lady doesn't need to explain herself. Traditionally the rate is half of the rack rate, and you have to check out by 6 p.m., but this varies by hotel, so be sure to ask in advance. "Some people don't even ask for the Day Use rate, but they only stay a few hours," said one bemused hotel manager. "Maybe they are too embarrassed to ask, but it's not as if we don't realize what they're doing."

INDEPENDENT LADIES

You're here to awaken your sensuality and embrace your sexiness.

A Note for Solo Adventurers

Central, safe, and welcoming are obvious qualities a woman on her own should look for in a hotel. One with its own restaurant can provide a great stand-by dining option when you don't want to venture far after dark, and solo females may feel more comfortable at the hotel bar enjoying a glass of wine or mingling with other travelers rather than braving a random bar elsewhere. Forget the bargain basement dives on this trip. You're here to awaken your sensuality and embrace your sexiness, which can't be done if you have bed bugs or moldy bathrooms. You need a cozy, decadent cocoon. A place to prepare the psyche — as well as the body — for another day or night on the town. A place where you wake up feeling like a true *Parisienne*.

Plaza Athénée (25 avenue Montaigne, 8ᵗʰ. Tel 01 53 67 66 65, fax 01 53 67 66 66. www.plaza-athenee-paris.com): Best place to pretend you're an internationally renowned sex columnist from New York. If you don't find your Mr. Big in the lobby or the trendy hotel bar, you can always console yourself in the neighboring couture boutiques.

Four Seasons George V (31 avenue George V, 8ᵗʰ. Tel 01 49 52 70 00, fax 01 49 52 70 10. www.fourseasons.com/paris): Best place to pretend you're Marie-Antoinette. The sumptuous spa recalls the queen's happier days being pampered in Versailles. When you're not lounging by the pool (strictly reserved for hotel guests only), settle into a prime people watching table overlooking the courtyard for a bit of afternoon tea…and cake?

Hôtel d'Aubusson (33 rue Dauphine, 6ᵗʰ. Tel 01 43 29 43 43, fax 01 43 29 12 62. www.hoteldaubusson.com): Best place to experience the jazz revival of the historic St-Germain-des-Prés district. By day, wander the Left Bank's lively maze of streets hiding fabulous bistros, independent cinemas and book shops. By night, strike an intellectual pose at the hotel's cozy Café Laurent for the live jazz performances.

Hotel Daniel (8 rue Frédéric Bastiat, 8th. Tel 01 42 56 17 00, fax 01 42 56 17 01. www.hoteldanielparis.com): Best place to pretend you're actually living in Paris. Make yourself at home amongst sumptuous fabrics and antique furnishings from France, North Africa, and the Far East. Rooms have *toile de Jouy* fabrics, lavender sachets and padded hangers in the closets, and glass jars of sea salts in the Moroccan-tiled bathrooms.

Hôtel Thérèse (5-7, rue Thérèse, 1st. Tel 01 42 96 10 01, fax 01 42 96 15 22. www.hoteltherese.com): Best place for discerning ladies on a budget. You'll hardly feel like a penny-pincher in this chic *quartier*, home to the Louvre, the Palais Royal, the Opéra Garnier and the exquisite Place Vendôme. Rooms here exude quality and understated chic, with crisp lines, soothing palettes, and must-have amenities such as air-conditioning and WiFi.

Gentleman Callers?

Perhaps you don't plan on staying solo very long. In that case, there's no need to be sneaky about bringing your new Parisian beau back to your room. The unwritten rule regarding discretion – both yours and the hotel staff's – will be respected. Just don't give them reason to think you're "working" – a lady doesn't have a revolving door into her bedroom. And don't forget to hang the "Ne pas deranger" sign on the door.

WHAT TO PACK

> *The sexiest thing in your wardrobe should be your attitude.*

Solo Getaways

• When choosing your clothes, try channeling the spirit of Audrey Hepburn: slim pants, simple top, ballet flats, scarf and sunglasses. If it's chilly, add a soft cardigan or classic trench coat to the list. Above all, your travel wardrobe should be chic, yet comfortable and — most important — mobile. You don't want to be slowed down by fussy ensembles or unreasonable shoes. Save the micro minis and macro-cleavage for the Bahamas. When you're solo, the sexiest thing in your wardrobe should be your attitude. You want to be mysterious sexy, not sexy "va va va voom!"

• A silky eyeshade for sleeping in late.

• An elegant journal and fountain pen for recording your adventures.

• Calling cards. Bonus points if you've had them made especially for your trip. Much more elegant than scribbling your e-mail on a Metro ticket stub.

• A stylish hat for bad hair days. Good ones form a triple barrier to the sun, rain, and chilly air.

• If you don't have anything to wear, pack an empty suitcase — you'll need room to bring home all of the treasures you find in Paris!

A Trip with the Gals

• You can dress more fun and flirty when you're traveling with the pack. There's a certain amount of safety in numbers. And hopefully your best friend will let you know when the hem of your skirt is tucked into your waistband.

• Essential: fabulous dancing shoes and at least one slinky dress.

• A digital camera and lots of backup storage! Remember: What happens in Paris, stays in Paris. But it's good to have some collateral later when you've accidentally spilled red wine all over your friend's cashmere sweater.

• If you come in the summer, bring a classy bathing suit for lounging at *Paris Plage*. Think French Riviera, not Atlantic City.

• Sexy short-shorts if you plan on joining a pole-dancing class.

For You and Your Man

• Pretend you're packing a wardrobe for your favorite big-screen heroine. Better to be overdressed in Paris than underdressed, especially when you see what the competition is wearing.

• All of the fabulous shoes you can only wear when you have a man's arm to steady you (preferably a man who knows how to hail a cab).

• Nothing but the most exquisite lingerie you own. Don't have any? Then bring none and exclaim at the hotel, "Oh my! I totally forgot to pack panties!" After he's completed a thorough strip search to verify this fact, lead him (and his Platinum card) to the nearest lingerie boutique (see the **Sexy You** chapter for addresses).

• If you've gone the "sexy slumming" route of budget accommodations, bring some decent candles or bath salts to erase any unpleasant scents that may be lingering.

• Extra scarves: use them to throw over any overly-bright lights in your hotel room, or to tie your naughty playmate to the bed (*bonus*: scarves don't show up in airport x-ray machines like handcuffs do).

• If your hotel room is equipped with a CD player, bring along a custom mix of sexy music for instant ambience (and to drown out any distracting sounds coming from adjacent rooms). Look to the naughty French rocker Serge Gainsbourg for local inspiration.

No One Should Leave Home Without

Do bring any and all "sexual health" products that you usually use. Traveling is not necessarily the best time to find out that you're allergic to latex or that your favorite lubricant isn't sold abroad. And you may not want to test the strength of your French at the local pharmacy (the only place where condoms are easily found) before testing out the hotel bed. If birth control is an issue, don't forget it! The Pill is available by prescription only in France. Turn to the Resource Guide for some handy vocabulary tips.

PART III

Sexy You

Sexy? Moi? Mais oui!

> *Being sexy is more of an attitude than a look of airbrushed perfection.*

And don't you believe for a moment that sexiness is about being vulgar, cheap, flashy, or otherwise unladylike. Despite lingering media stereotypes that try to convince us otherwise, the secret to being a sexy woman has nothing to do with Botox, silicone, liposuction, bleached teeth or revealing clothing.

At least not in Paris

Here in the City of Light, the sexiest women are the ones who look like they're not even trying. Self-assured, intriguing, captivating… it might seem like they're born this way, but Parisian women know that being sexy is more of an attitude than a superficial look of flaunted sexuality or airbrushed perfection. Their confidence comes from being raised in a culture that largely values femininity, elegance, wit and individual style.

French men are hardly immune to the charms of traditional good looks, despite novelist Marcel Proust's oft-quoted declaration, "Let us leave pretty women to men devoid of imagination." But they certainly have more open-minded views on what is considered attractive. There is even a celebrated phrase, *jolie-laide* (literally "pretty ugly"), describing unconventionally beautiful women whose flaws actually enhance their allure. In France, having asymmetrical features can be "interesting", but any obvious efforts at trying to look impressive for others will simply comes across as shallow. This may explain why Parisian women prefer to cultivate an aura of unintentional sexiness.

A girl should be two things: classy and fabulous.
– COCO CHANEL

That does not mean beauty and fashion are mere trivialities. *Au contraire!* This is Paris, after all. Ladies here spend as much time on their appearance as anyone else, but they are doing it first and foremost for themselves. In France, self-pampering and careful attention to personal style are considered essential elements of well being. And Parisian women know that if they look good, they'll feel good. Never underestimate what a facial and a fabulous bra can do to put a swing in your step and a naughty grin on your face!

There are many ways to coax your inner *femme fatale* out of hibernation. A sensual massage could reacquaint you with your body. The right outfit might awaken an alter ego. And a bit of shameless self indulgence may perhaps be the very key that unlocks your long-forgotten passion for life.

But no matter what road leads you to your sensual awakening, remember that it's about bringing out an undiscovered aspect of your true self, not trying to be someone you're not. Trust your women's intuition. And do what works for you. You'll know you're on the right track if you feel liberated, powerful, and – *oh là là* – even a bit naughty!

SPAS

> *The French idea of beauty is more about looking good from the inside out...*

Every goddess likes to be bathed and buffed and rejuvenated before facing the outside world. Begin your adventure in Paris with a precious beauty ritual that women have been performing since ancient times... a hot soak or steam bath, a thorough scrub, and a penetrating massage with essential oils. This powerful symbolic cleansing is the perfect way to leave behind the stresses of travel and your everyday life "back home" and emerge transformed as an intriguing and sensual international lady of mystery!

Note: With the right products and a large bath tub you can do this at your hotel, but there's something more indulgent (read: naughty) about having someone else do it for you!

GEORGE V SPA

FOUR SEASONS GEORGE V
31 AVENUE GEORGE V, 8TH.
TEL 01 49 52 70 00
M° GEORGE V
WWW.FOURSEASONS.COM/PARIS/

Bonjour, Your Highness. The crystal and marble grandeur is impressive, *oui*, but she needed to escape all of that. Marie-Antoinette preferred the intimate and luxurious setting of her Petite Trianon, beyond the gardens of Versailles, where she could relax far from Louis XVI's court and its tedious etiquette. Our discerning queen would have felt right at home in the heavenly-scented spa of the George V, with its delicate furnishings in creamy colors, real Toiles de Jouy fabrics padding the walls, and pale marble columns. The lights are dimmed under lampshades, the air delicately perfumed, and all sounds and stresses of the outside world completely muffled. Beyond the lounge, a large bay window overlooks a pool and hot tub surrounded by *trompe l'oeil* murals of Versailles' gardens. Reserve the VIP room, with double massage tables, private Jacuzzi and sauna, for a royal *rendez-vous à deux*, or bliss out in the relaxation room with your own personal music headphones. The pool and fitness room are reserved for the sole pleasure of the George V Hotel guests, but visitors can schedule the delicious spa packages (from €275). Discover Marie-Antoinette's secret beauty treatments or get wrapped in real Swiss chocolate! Over a dozen facials available, from €130.

LA MAISON GUERLAIN

68 AVENUE DES CHAMPS-ELYSÉES, 8TH.
M° GEORGE V
TEL 01 45 62 11 21
WWW.GUERLAIN.FR

When Guerlain opened its doors in 1912, the Champs Elysées was truly one of the most beautiful avenues in the world. Modernization *oblige*, the Maison Guerlain is one of the last remaining vestiges of this historic glamour. Step back in time into the opulent boutique of marble and crystal, where Parisian ladies have been purchasing their bottles of *Shalimar* and *Eau de Cologne Impériale* for almost a century. Ascend the elegant staircase, through a sea of glittering gold mosaic tiles, to the contemporary cosmetics and perfume ateliers. Here the make-over experts can show you how to achieve that Parisian look of "natural" beauty. A separate door leads to the spa, where Guerlain's sensuous elixirs — made from the most noble, rare and active ingredients — will make your skin (and *monsieur's* as well) as soft and smooth as silk from head to toe (facials from €90). Book the mythical "Cocooning Impériale" for a full day of intense pampering by the efficient, white-coated beauticians (€630).

French Savoir-Faire

The French idea of beauty is more about looking good from the inside out, so they focus their best expertise on skin care and body treatments rather than on more surface-level beauty services such as cosmetics and manicures. You can't go wrong with the remarkable variety and quality of their facials, among the most advanced in the industry, with specially targeted treatments for everything from jetlag and wrinkles to under-eye circles and blemishes. Cellulite removal treatments through lymphatic drainage massages and endermology – a French invention – are also widely available and affordable in Paris. Hair removal is another French forté, with many options at surprisingly affordable rates. When you want to put yourself completely in the hands of the experts, these services are where you should put your money. **

L'APPARTEMENT 217

217 RUE ST-HONORÉ, 1ST.
M° TUILERIES
TEL 01 42 96 00 96
WWW.LAPPARTEMENT217.COM

You're a woman who believes in natural beauty and a nurturing, healthy environment. Seek out this discreet entrance, through large wooden doors on a stylish shopping street, then up to the third floor, where you'll find this spa in a typically 19th-century apartment with the original parquet floors, marble fireplace mantels, and molded ceilings. These gracious historical details are harmoniously mixed, under the principals of Feng Shui, with soothing colors and comfortable furnishings for a calm and relaxed environment. You'll be served a freshly squeezed glass of juice, then wrapped up in a silky soft kimono made of organic pine-fiber and treated to a facial using Dr Hauschka's holistic skin products. At the end of your blissful 90-minute or two-hour facial, which includes a hand and foot massage (from €150), you'll feel like a new woman… *naturellement*.

GLOWING ROOM BY TERRY

10, AVENUE VICTOR HUGO, 16TH.
M° CHARLES DE GAULLE - ETOILE
TEL 01 55 73 00 73
WWW.BYTERRY.COM

Perhaps you, like the darling of the French cosmetics world Terry de Gunzburg, loathe the clinical atmosphere of typical beauty spas. Then you will surely feel right at home in her unique beauty parlor, created in 2007, without a sterile white wall in sight. Feel the plush chocolate carpeting under your toes, draw the taffeta curtains closed, and sink into the comfort of this jewel-toned "Glowing Room" adorned with Art Déco and Pop Art finds. Terry focuses on bringing out the natural beauty of the skin, so facials include detoxifying, hydrating and brightening treatments that make your skin feel like a baby's bottom (90-minute facials from €130). The exclusive By Terry cosmetics line is available in the boutique.

Tip: Try to book spa treatments as far in advance as possible, preferably before you arrive in Paris, to avoid disappointment.

Jean-François Duvigneau

34 RUE DAUPHINE, 6TH.
Mº ODEON
TEL 01 44 07 04 97

Are your thighs a bit too reminiscent of orange peels for your liking? Parisian ladies swear by endermology. Fortunately, these cellulite treatments are relatively affordable in France (about €75 per session), and physical therapist Jean-François is considered one of the best. His discreet *cabinet*, located in the St-Germain-des-Prés district, is modern yet soothing, with exposed brick walls. English spoken.

Les Bains du Marais

31 RUE DES BLANCS MANTEAUX, 4TH.
Mº RAMBUTEAU
TEL 01 44 61 02 02
WWW.LESBAINSDUMARAIS.COM

Terra cotta floors, wrought iron details and mosaic tiles evoke the mood of traditional Mediterranean steam baths. Give yourself at least a half day to luxuriate, alternating sessions in the hot steam rooms with cooling showers, vigorous body scrubs or private massages. Upstairs, the hip and trendy clientele congregate in the relaxed spa café. The services of a full-service beauty spa are available, including hair, nails, facials, waxing, and even tanning beds, but the steam baths are the real draw (from €35). Come alone or with your friends on the women-only days, or enjoy the steamy atmosphere with your man on mixed days (bathing suits required, *bien sûr*).

Le Hammam de la Mosquée

39 RUE SAINT-HILAIRE, 5TH.
M° CENSIER-DAUBENTON
TEL 01 43 31 38 20
WWW.LA-MOSQUEE.COM

The pleasures of Paris are not uniquely French in origin. *Au contraire*, this cosmopolitan city also offers the adventurous visitor many exotic delights, such as the stunning Paris Mosque, built in 1920 for the city's predominantly Algerian, Tunisian, and Moroccan Muslim community. Beyond the towering minaret are flowering courtyards, elaborate mosaic tiling, and soothing fountains recalling the Spanish Alhambra. The tearoom, restaurant and authentic *hammam* (steam baths) are open to the public (from €15). Unlike the quietly formal setting of typical French spas, women go to the *hammam* to socialize in a sisterly, laid-back atmosphere. Go with your lady friends and join in the convivial, centuries-old tradition!

How to Hammam: The process can be confusing, so follow the lead of the other women. Bathing suits (at least bottoms) are required, although robes, towels, sandals and even loofah mitts can be rented for a small fee. Your forfait entry fee (€38) includes access to the two steam rooms and cold plunge pool, a thorough body scrub (using black soap, or savon noir), and an oil massage. Do keep in mind that the hygiene standards are the same you might expect in an 88-year-old public swimming pool! When you're done, wrap up in a towel and hang out in the lounge with a glass of hot mint tea. Reservations aren't necessary (call for women's hours), but avoid crowded Saturdays.

What could be more beautiful than a dear old lady growing wise with age?
Every age can be enchanting, provided you live within it.

—BRIGITTE BARDOT

COSMETICS AND PERFUME

How to expertly emulate that "natural-yet-polished" look...

Paris will delight you with the sheer number boutiques devoted solely to the world of cosmetics and perfume. Who cares if your *boudoir* is already overflowing with beauty products back home? Spoil yourself with sparkly new cosmetics in pretty cases, a scandalous pair of false eyelashes, or a tube of truly red lipstick that will have you saying, *"Moi,* a Soccer Mom?" Of course, for everyday elegance, Parisians would never want to look like they're actually wearing makeup, *quelle horreur!* Most cosmetic boutiques offer lessons on how to expertly emulate that "natural-yet-polished" look that suits ladies of all ages.

Most women already know that scent can be one of the most powerful triggers of emotions and memories. You may be the kind of woman who has been wearing a classic signature scent for years, or a woman who changes her perfumes with the seasons like fashion. In either case, we invite you to leave these behind when you travel to Paris. A new scent is a must! Treat yourself to a leisurely afternoon seeking out the perfect new *eau de parfum* – something completely different and unforgettable – that will forever remind you of Paris!

Théâtre de la Beauté

LE BON MARCHÉ
24 RUE DE SÈVRES, 7TH.
Mº SÈVRES-BABYLONE
TEL 01 44 39 80 00
WWW.LEBONMARCHE.FR

Parisians are not impressed with the ubiquitous hoards that crowd the beauty counters of the Right Bank department stores. Those in the know prefer the more refined experience of shopping at Le Bon Marché, the historic department store on the Rive Gauche. *Le Théâtre de la Beauté* is indeed a sort of theatre, occupying center stage, its alluring collection of cosmetics, perfumes and skincare visible from every floor as you shop: Hermès, Chanel, Dior, Shu Uemura, Creed, Alexandre de Paris, Armani, La Prairie, Carita, Decléor…be sure to ask about exclusivities and limited editions that are unavailable back home.

Naughty Note

Perhaps you, like most Parisian women, prefer to reserve the ruby red lipstick for special occasions. But you can also use it to seal your naughty Paris postcards with a kiss!

MAISON CALAVAS

13 RUE ROYAL, 2ND FLOOR, 8TH.
M° CONCORDE OR MADELEINE
TEL 01 40 07 57 57
WWW.MAISONCALAVAS.FR

Someday your grandchildren will hold this precious cosmetics case of 24-carat gold and patent crocodile in their hands, thinking how glamorous your life must have been. "She got this in Paris!" And not just anywhere in Paris, but in the 18th-century townhouse designed by Louis XV's architect, its carefully-preserved décor a magnificent setting for the made-to-measure, limited edition cosmetics cases of the Maison Calavas. Choose from luxury leathers, snake skins, sting ray…then select the custom cosmetics palette and brushes that will complete your treasured beauty *trousse*. Expensive, *oui*, but consider it an investment the legend of your life.

LES SALONS DU PALAIS ROYAL SHISEIDO

JARDINS DU PALAIS ROYAL
142 GALERIE DE VALOIS, 1ST.
TEL 01 49 27 09 09
WWW.SALONS-SHISEIDO.COM

Stroll through the serene gardens of the Palais Royal, passing beneath the ancient stone arcades to the *jardin secret* of Serge Lutens, Shiseido's artisan perfumer. This enchanting jewel-box of a boutique is a violet boudoir where his luxury scents are lovingly displayed for your leisurely perusal. Try the orange blossom, the incense and lavender, the amber… or dare the tuberose "criminelle", the night rose. Have your initials – or *his?* – engraved on the elegant glass bottle. Serge creates 60 limited edition bottles every Christmas. You'll just *have* to come back to Paris for refills, won't you?

Essential Naughty Flirting Accessory

Every lady with naughty inclinations should own a pretty little compact mirror. Please, leave the ugly plastic one in your gym bag. Not only is a compact mirror handy for reapplying lipstick or spotting a bit of chocolate on the corner of your mouth, it's also the perfect flirting accessory. Be discreet and check him out when he thinks your back is turned. Be naughty by giving him a wink when he catches you!

EDITIONS DE PARFUMS

37 RUE DE GRENELLE, 7TH.
M° RUE DU BAC
TEL 01 42 22 76 40.
WWW.EDITIONSDEPARFUMS.COM

Your man wouldn't be caught dead in a flowery perfume boutique. Bring him here, and just watch his resistance crumble as he enters Frédéric Malle's distinctly masculine couture house of perfume. Wood paneled walls, polished concrete floors, contemporary art and retro curiosities… and did we mention the futuristic gadgets? The smelling column, a glass compartment that just might beam you up, allows you to fully experience the 16 perfect scents created by Frédéric and his nine perfumers, *les nez*. The actual perfumes, for both men and women, are kept in refrigerated glass cabinets until purchased. *Two other addresses at 140 ave Victor Hugo, 16th, and 21 rue Mont Thabor, 1st.*

Libre Etat d'Orange

69 RUE DES ARCHIVES, 3RD.
M° RAMBUTEAU
TEL 01 42 78 30 09
WWW.ETATLIBREDORANGE.COM

It is sad to grow old but nice to ripen.
—*BRIGITTE BARDOT*

Enter the temple of naughty perfumes, where the *gentille* hostess presents you with scents that evoke the most vivid fantasies: "Putain des Palaces" (Palace Hotel Whore), "Rien" (Nothing), Jasmin et Cigarettes," "Sécretions Magnifiques" (Magnificent Secretions),"Vierges et Toreros" (Virgins and Bullfighters) and perfumed candles such as "Bottes et Ceinturon" (Boots and Belt). And in case the French title wasn't suggestive enough, each scent has a cheeky little image to go with it. The boutique, decorated with daring neo-baroque furnishings by Serge Olivares, also presents a saucy selection of Taschen coffee table books, including art, travel and photography guides.

Hair & Nails

> *Nothing is sexier than loose parts and tousled bangs hanging in your eyes.*

Caveat Emptor!

As for your heavenly tresses, hold onto your hairbrush before going overboard. The French have a very different idea of how a woman's mane should look. In keeping with the illusion of effortless and natural beauty, they would never want an over-polished "fresh from the salon" style. Parisians would love you to think that they just rolled out of bed and ran a hand through their glossy hair before gliding out the door. They think nothing is sexier than loose parts and tousled bangs hanging in your eyes. It can be a liberating style if you can pull it off. But if you prefer a severe bob or a sculpted coiffure à la Catherine Deneuve, best come armed with photos to overcome any language barriers. But be forewarned: your headstrong "we know what's best" Parisian stylist may completely ignore it and give you the cut they prefer anyway, *mon dieu*!

For those who would rather steer clear of the snippers, you can still have your hair styled for a night on the town. Nothing feels more luxuriously naughty than a French "brushing." An expert turn of the hairdryer and a strategically-placed pin or two, *et voila*! You've got a sexy updo that would make Brigitte Bardot proud!

LA NOUVELLE ATHÈNES

1 RUE DE LIÈGE, 9TH.
M° LIÈGE
TEL 01 48 74 86 89
WWW.LANOUVELLEATHENES.COM

Sylvie Coudray's *Atelier de Coiffure* is not a typical hair salon. You have to know the address, press the buzzer to announce your arrival, and then take the old-fashioned elevator up to a traditional bourgeois Parisian apartment. Tall windows overlook the street, delicate molding surrounds vintage mirrors, a cat lounges in one corner, and sultry jazz plays quietly on the stereo. Nothing sterile or industrial here! Sink into one of the antique armchairs with a café to relax while Sylvie and her team prepare to take care of you like an old friend. English with a charming French accent spoken here! Color, brows, extensions and makeovers are available, but the real magic is in the custom cuts, designed to not only suit your face and lifestyle, but to work with the natural inclination of your own hair. More affordable than you'd guess, with shampoo-cut-blow dry from €65. Bring cash.

ALEXANDRE ZOUARI

1 AVENUE DU PRESIDENT WILSON, 16TH.
M° ALMA-MARCEAU
TEL 01 47 23 79 00
WWW.ALEXANDRE-ZOUARI.COM

You would rather "see and be seen," and you're willing to pay for that luxury. Then book yourself an afternoon of pampering at the Alexandre Zoari salon, strategically located on the border of the swank 8th and 16th arrondissements. Your hotel concierge may be able to get you an appointment with Monsieur Z himself, otherwise you are in the capable hands of his crack team for hair, nails, facials and massages. Facial, haircut and manicure packages are available from €300, and include a healthy lunch and prime people-watching opportunities.

AUTOUR DE CHRISTOPHE ROBIN

9 RUE GUÉNÉGAUD, 6TH
M° ODÉON
TEL 01 42 60 99 15
WWW.COLORIST.NET

Do you demand the best of the best at any price? Put your tresses in the expert hands of Christophe Robin, one of the most sought-after hair colorists in the world. His techniques not only enhance your hair's body and shine, but also flatter your skin tone and make your eyes sparkle (from €300-€600). Christophe's chic Left Bank salon is also home to a team of talented hair, skin and nail experts, including pedicurist-to-the -stars Bastien Gonzalez, whose exclusive medical pedicure and in-depth massage will completely transform your tootsies (from €120). Forget about a last-minute *rendez-vous*. Book your appointment here before you've even purchased your ticket to Paris!

MANUCURIST SAINT HONORÉ

42 PLACE DU MARCHÉ ST HONORÉ, 1ST.
M° TUILERIES
TEL 01 42 61 03 81
www.manucurist.com

When visiting Paris, don't expect to find the same inexpensive walk-in nail salons that you see on every corner in New York and Los Angeles. Although the American concept of colorful, high-maintenance nails has definitely crossed the Atlantic, it's still considered more of a fad than a necessity for the average Parisian woman. Manucurist is one of the few nail bars in the city that specialize in the American-style manicure techniques, including UV gels, silk wraps and fiberglass extensions. Simple polish change starts at €18, full manicures from €32, and spa manicures from €45. Call a day in advance to make an appointment. Two other locations at Opéra (13 rue de la Chaussée d Antin, 9th, tel 01 47 03 37 33) and Madeleine (4 rue de Castellane, 8th, tel 01 42 65 19 30).

Extra Naughty Note

You don't have to be a professional dancer to enjoy the surprisingly smooth and streamlined sensation of a Brazilian bikini wax, or epilation maillot brésilien, which removes virtually all of the "intimate" hair aside from a tiny triangle, including any strays entre fesses for superfuzzy ladies. And no one else needs to know why there's an extra slink in your step as you saunter through the streets of Paris. The luxury spas all offer bikini waxing, but you can also have it done in any neighborhood institut de beauté for about €30.

The "Real" French Manicure

Did you know that the famous two-toned French Manicure was actually invented in Hollywood in 1974? The style's creator, American makeup artist Jeff Pink, was inspired by the Parisian runway models who simply rubbed a white pencil beneath their unvarnished nails for a clean, high-contrast effect. You can certainly get the "French Manicure" and classic colored varnish in salons, but most Parisians still prefer an elegant and unfussy natural look – buffed and shiny nails that are not too long, lightly rounded, and immaculately clean.

BODY ART

Create a lasting memory of your trip to Paris...

Morgan is a strikingly beautiful woman from Colorado, married with children. For her 40th birthday she decided to treat herself to a trip to Paris with her best friend. But that's not all she treated herself to. "There's something you need to know about married suburban American women," she confided. "When we turn 40 we do one -- or all -- of the following: get a tattoo, pierce the belly button, have a lesbian experience, have an affair, or have erotic nude photos of ourselves taken." Morgan's secret will remain a secret, *bien sûr.* But you, too, can create a lasting memory of your trip to Paris, at any age.

There are many reputable tattoo, piercing and body art boutiques in Paris. Here are just two recommendations:

ABRAXAS

9 RUE SAINT MERRI, 4TH.
Mº HÔTEL DE VILLE
TEL: 01 48 04 33 55
WWW.ABRAXAS.FR

The crack team of corporal artists at Abraxas specialize in all types of body piercing (including "intimate" areas) and tattoos. Their stylish boutique looks more like a jewelry store than a purveyor of pain, so you'll feel immediately at ease. Their second location (5 rue du Marché Saint-Honoré, 1st, Tel 01 40 15 62 20) also does henna tattoos and permanent make-up.

FLORENCE AMBLARD ATELIER

25 RUE DE BELFORT, 11TH.
Mº VOLTAIRE
TEL 01 43.48 78 05
WWW.FLORENCE-AMBLARD.COM

Looking for a real Parisian work of art? Florence is a French painter who once lived in San Francisco. She spent two years in Tahiti, where she learned how to transform her surrealist artworks into beautiful tattoos. Today her whimsical tattoo parlor is located discreetly in the back of her mosaic-tiled Parisian art gallery, where she creates custom designs for each client in her unique style.

WHAT TO WEAR?!

The focus should be on you,
not your clothing.

If you're already one seriously stylish lady, then Paris is your playground. Enjoy! But if the words "Parisian fashion" make you quake in your baggy khaki's, then never fear, help is here. Women of any age and body type can capture the essence of French flair by following these three useful wardrobe guidelines:

* It must look good on **you**. Parisians only adopt the latest trends if they flatter their own personal body type. If you don't know which styles suit you, enlist a fashion consultant or your most stylish friends for an honest appraisal.
* It must **feel** good. Choose properly fitting, well-cut items in high-quality fabrics, especially when buying coats, jackets and suits. A few quality pieces are worth more than a wardrobe full of cheap, ill-fitting clothes.
* Keep it **simple**. Parisians wear black because it's slimming, timeless, simple to coordinate, and easy to care for. You should also know which neutral tones like grey, beige, chocolate or navy look best with your skin and hair color.

Wearing comfortable, flattering, and timeless classics will make you feel good. And you ladies know that when you feel good, you can't help but look confident and, *quelle surprise*, sexy! After all, the focus should be on you, not your clothing.

Cross-Channel Fashion *Faux Pas*

"You can spot an English girl out on the razz a mile off in Paris," laments British fashion writer Rebecca Catt. "The f***-me boots and mini skirts act as instant clues. Low cut tops and the (oft misguided) lack of coat to cover up are also dead giveaways. At home we're used to trundling out half dressed – no queues for the cloakroom – with tiny handbags for the bare essentials."

A dress makes no sense unless it inspires men to take it off of you.
—FRANCOISE SAGAN

Suivez-moi, jeune homme!

This oft-used French phrase (usually written as suivez-moi-jeune-homme) literally means "follow me, young man." It refers to a ribbon tied around a lady's hat which dangles down to the neck. In the 19th century, women, especially married women, wore a suivez-moi-jeune-homme as a discreet invitation to men. What a shame that this phrase went out of fashion with ribboned hats!

ADVICE FROM PETITE BRIGITTE

Look like a million without looking like you care.

You won't be able to fool the eagle-eyed Parisians into thinking you're one of them, but you'll gain their respect and admiration if, as with the language, you make an honest effort. Undercover fashion and celebrity writer-about-town Petite Brigitte knows the secret to achieving *le look Parisien*.

Not only is this look surprisingly easy for anyone to achieve, it's also inherently sexy without ever being trashy. There's something unmistakably naughty about the way Parisian ladies manage to turn up their sexual voltage without even appearing to try!

> *A woman is closest to being naked*
> *when she is well-dressed.*
> —COCO CHANEL

"What comes across as sexy and attractive in Paris is a distinct *mélange* of artless elegance," says Petite Brigitte. "The trick is look like a million without looking like you care. Parisian society shuns those who look *nouveau riche!*" Some basic no-no's include wearing trendy logos, too many bright colors, and heavy make-up. Watch a few French films, and you'll see the heroines usually have a more "natural" look than the every-hair-in-place perfection of Hollywood's ice queens.

"The ladies-who-lunch crowd can be found wearing skinny jeans with heels or ballerina flats, big cashmere sweaters, and artfully disheveled hair." She recommends one or two subtle details to add the desired look of understated wealth, such as a Cartier watch or oversized Chanel bag. "By night, these mysterious vixens will have transformed into *femme fatales*, but again, nothing too flashy or overtly sexual."

Petite Brigitte's Wardrobe Must-Haves

- Silk or cashmere scarf
- Little black dress
- Tailored white shirt
- Oversized tote bag for shopping
- Cashmere sweater

- Striped *marinière* sailor shirt
- Sexy, matching lingerie
- Flattering jeans in a dark rinse
- Shoes: a pair of heels, boots, and ballerinas

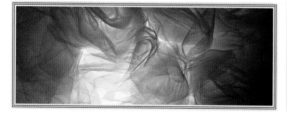

Classic Parisienne Style

Shopping anywhere in Paris is pure bliss, but finding truly special boutiques on a short time frame takes some insider knowledge. Here are some of Petite Brigitte's favorite classic haunts, to help you make the most of your short stay. These typically Parisian shops can be pricey, but remember... this is Paris. *C'est la vie!*

AZZEDINE ALAÏA

7 RUE DE MOUSSY, 4TH.
M° HÔTEL DE VILLE
TEL 01 42 72 19 19

The label of choice for Parisian femme fatales, from the editor of French Vogue to Catherine Deneuve. With the impeccable, form-fitting cuts and timeless style, women in Alaïa look sophisticated and untouchable, and undeniably sexy. *Note*: Savvy ladies will find last season's discounted stock at a hidden shop around the corner, 18 rue de la Verrerie.

ANNE FONTAINE

370 RUE ST-HONORÉ, 1ST.
M° CONCORDE
TEL 01 42 96 51 14

She's the reigning queen of the 'white shirt,' and boy does she know how to cut them! Anne Fontaine's boutique on the trendy rue St. Honoré is a timeless address in any Parisian's shopping diary, and now hosts a promising new spa on the lower levels. Whether you are in the market for an everyday shirt, or sophisticated evening elegance, this shop has every style you can imagine, with service that is helpful and friendly.

LE BON MARCHÉ

24 RUE DE SÈVRES, 7TH.
M° SÈVRES-BABYLONE
TEL 01 44 39 80 00
WWW.LEBONMARCHE.FR

Opened in 1838, the oldest department store in the world is still an institution in the Parisian fashion scene. It's smaller and more prestigious than other department stores, and showcases designers like Balenciaga, Rykiel, Westwood, and Rick Owens. Be sure to cross the upstairs breezeway which leads to lesser priced yet equally coveted selections by Zadig & Voltaire, Vanessa Bruno, and Mont St. Michel. There is also a hip moderately-priced restaurant called Delica'Bar, which serves incredible salads and tartelettes in a terrace setting. Bon Marché is one-stop fulfillment for the serious shopper of all budgets.

MONA

17 RUE BONAPARTE, 6TH.
M° SAINT GERMAIN DES PRÈS
TEL 01 44 07 07 27

DIDIER LUDOT

24, GALERIE MONTPENSIER, 1ST.
M° PALAIS ROYAL
TEL 01 42 96 06 56

Surrounded by galleries and the Ecole des Beaux-Arts, this exclusive boutique stocks a collection of the sexiest ensembles on the Left Bank. You will spot those hard-to-find shoes by Lanvin or Pierre Hardy, fall in love with bags by Bottega Veneta, and feel like a million bucks in a dress by Alexander McQueen. Flattering mirrors and kind salespeople make this an easy place to drop a pretty penny. This should be a definite stop on any stroll through the left bank, and number one on your list for the sales season, when everything is 50-70% off.

Many of us dream of looking like a film diva, but this is the only shop where you actually have the chance to buy authentic red-carpet ensembles. As the most famous vintage dealer in Paris, Ludot's shop overlooking the gorgeous Palais Royal gardens will have you gawking more than a trip to the Louvre. You'll find 1960's Givenchy dresses, Hermès bags, Chanel tweed blazers — all in immaculate condition, and with prices to match. It is always a pleasant stop after a long lunch in one of the shady cafés along the arcade. Cross the gardens to the second boutique, dedicated to that timeless wardrobe must-have: the little black dress.

A Note on Sales & Returns

In France, protectionist laws regulating the textile industry mean that clothing sales only take place twice annually, in January and August. And before you buy something you're not sure about, double check the returns policy, even outside the sales you may be issued a store credit rather than getting your money back.

PAUL & JOE

66 RUE DES SAINTS-PÈRES, 7TH.
Mᵒ SAINT GERMAIN DES PRÈS
TEL 01 42 22 13 08
WWW.PAULANDJOE.COM

Feminine, fresh, and classic. This is one shop where you will see mothers and daughters shopping side by side. Named after her two sons, designer Sophie Albou has redefined Parisian femininity with her easy-to-wear styles and lush colors. Walking into her boutique is like stepping into a Parisian dreamworld; the muted colors, unexpected details, and fine prints make multiple purchases almost inevitable. While her collections are rather good-girl in tone, they bring to mind Catherine Deneuve in "Belle de Jour"... and we recall just how naughty she ended up!

Fashion Insider News

Keep up with the latest Parisian fashion news on Petite Brigitte's blog spot, www.petitebrigitte.com

→ TRENDSETTER DU JOUR

Paris isn't just a city for classic beauty—it rivals New York and London for its share of eclectic labels and one-off boutiques featuring unique and edgy creations from around the world. Whether you are young, or just young at heart, these are stores that will get your heart racing and redefine your perception of French fashion.

Buyers Beware!

To borrow from the famous saying, regret for our impulsive purchases can be tempered by time; it's regret for the fabulous finds we left behind that is inconsolable. Nothing is more heartbreaking than the bittersweet memory of that perfect little hat, those exquisitely dainty sandals or that beautifully-cut dress that we decided we didn't need or couldn't afford. If the naughtiest thing you ever do in Paris is give into the temptation of conspicuous consumption, then do it proudly, without looking back. Carpé diem! →

COLETTE

213 RUE ST-HONORÉ, 1ST.
M° TUILERIES
TEL 01 55 35 33 90
WWW.COLETTE.FR

It's one of the most famous 'concept stores' in the world, and the store that you just can't miss (the crowds of people flocking inside ensure that as well). Let one of Colette's personal stylists take care of you, or just copy a look off of one of the ever-changing mannequins. The store showcases all of the fashion editors' top picks of the season, from Alaïa to Yamamoto. While it may seemed packed on the first floor (which is an addictive stop to check out new gadgets, music, and accessories), the crowds thin as you climb the stairs…so will your wallet.

LE 66

66 AVENUE DES CHAMPS-ELYSÉES, 8TH.
M° GEORGE V
TEL 01 53 53 33 80
WWW.LE66.FR

This clothing concept store is the newest addition to shopping on the Champs-Elysées. Nearly one hundred labels fill a massive underground space with men's and women's clothes for a variety of budgets. Clothes for day and night sit next to quirky shoe labels and killer accessories. The store synthesizes many home-grown Parisian labels, like BA&SH, Antik Batik, and Kiliwatch, along with some one-of-a-kind pieces from international labels. Don't miss the collection of rare DVD's, which includes some *risqué* vintage pornography!

MONTAIGNE MARKET

57 AVENUE MONTAIGNE, 8TH.
M° FRANKLIN D. ROOSEVELT
TEL 01 42 56 58 58

This multi-brand boutique on the most exclusive avenue in the city is an efficient way of perusing the latest from Yves Saint Laurent, Givenchy, and MiuMiu alongside more down-to-earth brands and rising designers from Paris, New York, and London. The boutique boasts a modern design and Zen vibe that highlights some colorful and exciting couture creations.

L'ECLAIREUR

29BIS RUE DES ROSIERS, 4TH.
M° ST-PAUL
TEL 01 44 78 81 81
WWW.LECLAIREUR.COM

You're virtually guaranteed to come away looking *hyper-sexy* and Parisian after shopping here. Cutting edge designers, edgy accessories, and a hip location in the Marais make this number one on any list. From accessories to shoes, the store is a little rock star, but oh-so *élégant*. Bring your beau to the men's store at the end of the street (12 rue Malher, 4th). A larger branch with its own bar is at 8 rue Boissy d'Anglas, 8th (tel 01 53 43 80 12) and a hidden location with exclusive brands can be found at 9 rue Hérold, 1st (tel 01 45 08 17 68, ring the buzzer for entry).

ZADIG & VOLTAIRE

9 RUE DU 29 JUILLET, 1ST.
TEL 01 42 92 00 80
WWW.ZADIG-ET-VOLTAIRE.COM

Zadig manages to make rock & roll look luxurious and classy. Known for their sexy cashmere sweaters, often emblazoned with single words like Happiness, Peace, or Elvis. You can also customize your sweater to say anything you want. The leather bags are popular thanks to good proportions and hip detailing. Their clothes are the perfect look for an afternoon spent people-watching in a café.

AMERICAN RETRO
40 RUE DES FRANCS-BOURGEOIS, 4TH.
M° ST-PAUL
TEL 01 42 78 42 40
WWW.AMERICANRETRO.FR

Don't let the name fool you: this boutique is all about French style. Created by two Parisian brothers, American Retro now has multiple boutiques around the city, but the most lively and enjoyable is found in the heart of the Marais shopping district. You will find specialty cashmeres, intricate embroidered dresses, and sexy heels from Parisian designer Gaspard Yurkievich. And while the vibe is a little retro, you'll come out looking *très* fashion forward.

Sexy on a Budget

Parisian ladies stretch their euros by mixing their designer threads with items from more mainstream chain shops such as Etam, Morgan, Zara, H&M, and Promod (hint: most of these can be found on the Rue de Rivoli between Hôtel de Ville and the Louvre).

OH LÀ LÀ LINGERIE

The right lingerie can lift more than your lovely female form. It can also lift your spirits, completely change the line of an outfit, and put you on even par with the Parisian ladies who wouldn't dare step out of the front door without a matching ensemble in impeccable condition. "Wearing matching lingerie not only makes you feel sexy (and naughty)," says *Two Lipsticks and a Lover* author, Helena Frith Powell. "But also, should a Frenchman get to your underwear and find it's non-matching, he may storm out of the bedroom." If you have nothing that fits this description, count yourself lucky. You get to go shopping!

CADOLLE

4 RUE CAMBON, 1ST.
Mº TUILERIES
TEL 01 42 60 94 22
WWW.CADOLLE.COM

Herminie Cadolle liberated women from the restraints of the corset in 1889 when she invented the bra. Legend has it that she even created a bra of metal and ribbon for the infamous spy Mata Hari. Ironic, perhaps, that today the brand is known for its made-to-order corsets, which Herminie's heirs reintroduced after World War I with the birth of Haute Couture. You'll find ready-to-wear corsets and lingerie at the Cadolle Boutique on rue Cambon. For a custom-made corset, call for a *rendez-vous* at Cadolle Loft Couture at 255 rue St-Honoré, 1st, tel 01 42 60 94 94.

YOBA

11, RUE DU MARCHÉ ST-HONORÉ, 1ST.
Mº TUILERIES
TEL 01 40 41 04 06
WWW.YOBAPARIS.COM

Yoba's bubblegum pink boutique is discreetly located on a quiet courtyard just off the chic Marché St-Honoré, accessible by pressing the silver button on the code panel outside the heavy wooden doors. One of the young ladies will buzz you into a bright and elegant boutique of parquet floors and crystal chandeliers, where you'll find an exquisite selection of dainty—yet naughty—lingerie designed to seduce, from silk triangle halters that outline the breasts to exquisite lace G-strings and matching bras that tie around the neck in a bow. And everything is of the highest quality, from the tear-away satin panties to the pastel feather boas. Yoba also sells silver vibrators, satin cuffs, erotic massage creams, and naughty books for ladies. Be sure to stop by during the Thursday evening "apéros coquins," a ladies-only Champagne reception where you can browse the latest collection in a festive atmosphere.

Nobody is young after forty years but one can be irresistible at any age
—COCO CHANEL

CHANTAL THOMASS

211 RUE ST-HONORÉ, 1ST.
M° TUILERIES
TEL 01 42 60 40 56
WWW.CHANTALTHOMASS.FR

LOUISE FEUILLÈRE

102 RUE DES DAMES, 17TH.
M° ROME
TEL 01 42 93 17 76
WWW.LOUISEFEUILLERE.COM

When everyone was wearing "practical" underwear back in the 70s, the black-bobbed Parisian designer Chantal Thomass reintroduced the feminine frills, smooth silks and sexy stockings that she's known for today. You simply can't come to Paris without visiting her pink padded burlesque boutique to fawn over the lacy garter belts, the corseted merry widows and naughty black seamed stocking. You'll also find sexy stilettos, scent diffusers, notebooks, naughty handheld fans, girly shopping bags, and the prettiest umbrellas that will have you looking forward to rainy days.

Made-to-measure corsets, sewn by hand on traditional sewing machines right here in France using the highest quality materials, according to the customer's own desires. You can also browse the ready-to-wear in the boutique, open Saturdays only. The prices here, perhaps from the off-the-beaten-track location and the refusal of the lady to do mass production, means that even budget-conscious ladies can afford to treat themselves. Custom orders by appointment only.

The Naughty Lingerie Check List

- A perfectly-fitted corset
- Demi-cup or push-up bra that creates a "balcony"
- Black seamed stockings
- Garter belt ensemble
- A long, silk night gown for elegant lounging
- Panties that can be whipped off
- A naughty, see-through babydoll
- A marabou-trimmed robe

AUBADE

25 RUE DANIELLE CASANOVA, 1ST.
M° PYRAMIDES
TEL 01 42 61 42 06
WWW.AUBADE.COM

Aubade's famously naughty "Lessons in Seduction" billboards have probably caused more than one car accident. Men can't resist the sight of the abundant breasts and beautiful bottoms decked out in classic, lacy lingerie, while we ladies appreciate the clever seduction tactics such as "Set the trap and wait," "Cultivate mystery," "Use hypnosis if he resists" and "Detour the conversation." You can find Aubade in most department stores, but their own boutiques, branded "'L'Art d'Aimer" (Art of Loving), carry the entire line as well as the sexy accessories such as the annual calendar and book of their famous lessons. Try the "soul mate" kit, the "Philtre d'Amour" roll-on perfume of six essential oils, or limited edition goo·lies like the Tarot de L'Amour tarot cards.

L'Industrie Lingerie

7 RUE SEDAINE, 11TH.
M° BASTILLE
TEL 01 47 00 41 19

All self-respecting *Parisiennes* know that the secret to assembling a fine collection of lingerie has more to do with savvy shopping than what tax bracket you fall into. Case in point: this tiny, neo-retro boutique with the whimsical fresco on the ceiling specializes in sexy, yet affordable bras, panties, teddies and nighties in just three colors — black, white, and red. A few naughty toys are tucked onto the shelves, and clients get 5% off all purchases if you've eaten at the popular Café de l'Industrie, across the street.

Also: You can find *très risqué* lingerie and naughty nightwear at Metamorph'Ose, Dollhouse, Nuits Blanche, and Amours Délices et Orgues *(see Naughty Shopping)*. For one-stop shopping, Parisian department stores Le Bon Marché and Le Printemps have all of the major lingerie brands attractively presented in one place.

Sexy Shoes

Only women can truly understand the shameless pleasure of treating ourselves to a new pair of fabulous shoes. Like chocolates and bodice-ripping romance novels, their very frivolity and decadence make them the ultimate naughty self-indulgence. You simply can't strut your sexy stuff without the right shoes. And nothing can transform a dress from so-so to sizzling faster than the click of your stiletto heels!

So how do you find the perfect shoes? You'll know they're meant for you if you feel giddy, can't stop jumping up and down, don't care that they cost more than your car, and fit like a glove. In other words, you must fall passionately in love with them! Forget practical, reasonable, and – *yawn* – sensible. You have enough of those in your closet already. When in doubt, stick with black and the highest heel you can manage without toppling into the Seine.

Note: Trendy sneakers may have snuck into the wardrobes of hipster Parisians, but they are not appropriate for any of the addresses in this guide, so leave them at home, s'il vous plait. Invest instead in a pair of stylish boots or dainty ballerinas à la Audrey Hepburn for daytime comfort sans frumpiness.

CHRISTIAN LOUBOUTIN

19 RUE JEAN-JACQUES ROUSSEAU, 1ST.
M° LOUVRE-RIVOLI
TEL 01 42 36 05 31
WWW.CHRISTIANLOUBOUTIN.FR

You could be wearing a conservative pants suit, but when those-in-the-know spot the signature red lacquered soles of your Christian Louboutin's, they'll know you're a lady with a naughty streak. Synonymous with sexy heels, Louboutin spent his formative years frequenting the music halls of Paris like the Folies Bergère, before perfecting his craft with industry legends Charles Jourdan and Roger Vivier. This is the original boutique, opened in 1992, where collections are usually presented according to heel height: high, higher, and *oh là là!* A more contemporary branch is located at 38 rue de Grenelle, 7th.

RODOLPHE MENUDIER

14 RUE CASTIGLIONE, 1ST.
M° TUILERIES
TEL 01 42 60 86 27
WWW.RODOLPHEMENUDIER.COM

The *avant-garde* designs of Rodolphe Menudier's shoes bestow each amazing pair with fetish object status. Often colorful, always remarkable, these shoes won't fail to attract attention. Shed your wallflower reputation for good! The sleek and sexy black and chrome boutique designed by Christophe Pillet is well worth a visit in its own right.

CHARLES JOURDAN

23 RUE FRANÇOIS 1ER, 8TH.
M° GEORGE V
TEL 01 47 20 81 28
WWW.CHARLES-JOURDAN.COM

Charles Jourdan became a world-renowned name when his dramatic heels accompanied Christian Dior's New Look in 1947. A favorite of fashion icons from Brigitte Bardot to Princess Diana, these shoes are still synonymous with fit, craftsmanship, and their chic and bold architectural style. Bring out your own inner fashion icon with a pair of the suede knee-high boots or sexy patent sling-backs.

Omigod, shoes!

Department stores such as Printemps, Galeries Lafayette and Bon Marché have all of the major brands of shoes in one place, but then you'd miss out on the personalized attention of the smaller boutiques and the joy of discovering Paris while you shop. One of the best concentrations of designer and luxury shoe boutiques can be found in the St-Germain-des-Prés district where the Rue du Dragon, Rue de Grenelle, Rue du Four, Rue du Vieux Colombier and Rue du Cherche Midi intersect. If you've got an eagle eye for good quality and are willing to sift through the cheaper Chinese imports, head to the wholesale shoe street, Rue Meslay (just off the Place de la République, 3rd). There are few big-name brands, but with patient persistence you can find excellent bargains on current and last-season shoes from French, Italian and Spanish designers.

Thigh-high stiletto boots, patent leather platforms, and your classic racy F***-Me Pumps can be found in the Naughty Shopping section of this guide.

PERSONAL SHOPPING CONSULTANTS

Capture that elusive French allure...

Fashion and beauty and shoes, oh my! If you're feeling overwhelmed by choice, or simply wish to make the most of your time while in Paris, why not invest in a little help from the pros? Personal shoppers will find you the clothes and accessories that fit with your style, size, and price range, while image consultants help you develop or update your own personal style, including wardrobe, hair and make-up.

Most department stores have personal shopping services for busy Parisians, but if you're looking for a complete makeover and wardrobe fix, put yourself in the hands of the flamboyant Josy Mermet and her expert team at Printemps. She has been helping bring out the "inner you" in clients for 30 years using a technique she calls Chromopsychology. After an hour-long interview, her artist will create a series of sketches with recommended hair style, make-up, colors, textures, and clothing shapes. These reasonably-priced sessions include personalized shopping recommendations from the immense Printemps collections. Don't miss the "Before/After" photos on her website.

Extra Naughty

If you want to immortalize your sexy self forever, why not pose for an erotic photo session with a pro? American-born photographer Stephen Zezza (www.stephenzezza.com) is known for his Paris fashion and portrait work, but those in the know (just tell him Naughty Paris sent you) can commission his keen eye for a private session at very reasonable rates.

LA MODE-LE CLUB

TEL 01 45 05 17 29
WWW.LAMODE-LECLUB.COM

Elegance is not the prerogative of those who have just escaped from adolescence, but of those who have already taken possession of their future.

—COCO CHANEL

Chic, Swiss-born image consultant Jacqueline Sablayrolles knows exactly how to help her international clientele capture that elusive French allure. After a thorough consultation, she carefully hand-picks the best hairdresser and make-up artist to suit your personality. Then, with her little black book of the best secret Paris addresses, she'll take you shopping in a chauffeured car for the right clothing and accessories (and Jacqueline doesn't accept commissions, so there's no pressure to purchase). At the end of the day you'll celebrate your Parisian transformation with a glass of Champagne. Half-day, full-day, and small group packages can be arranged (from €600), as well as specialty fashion tours and couture shows. Jacqueline speaks flawless English.

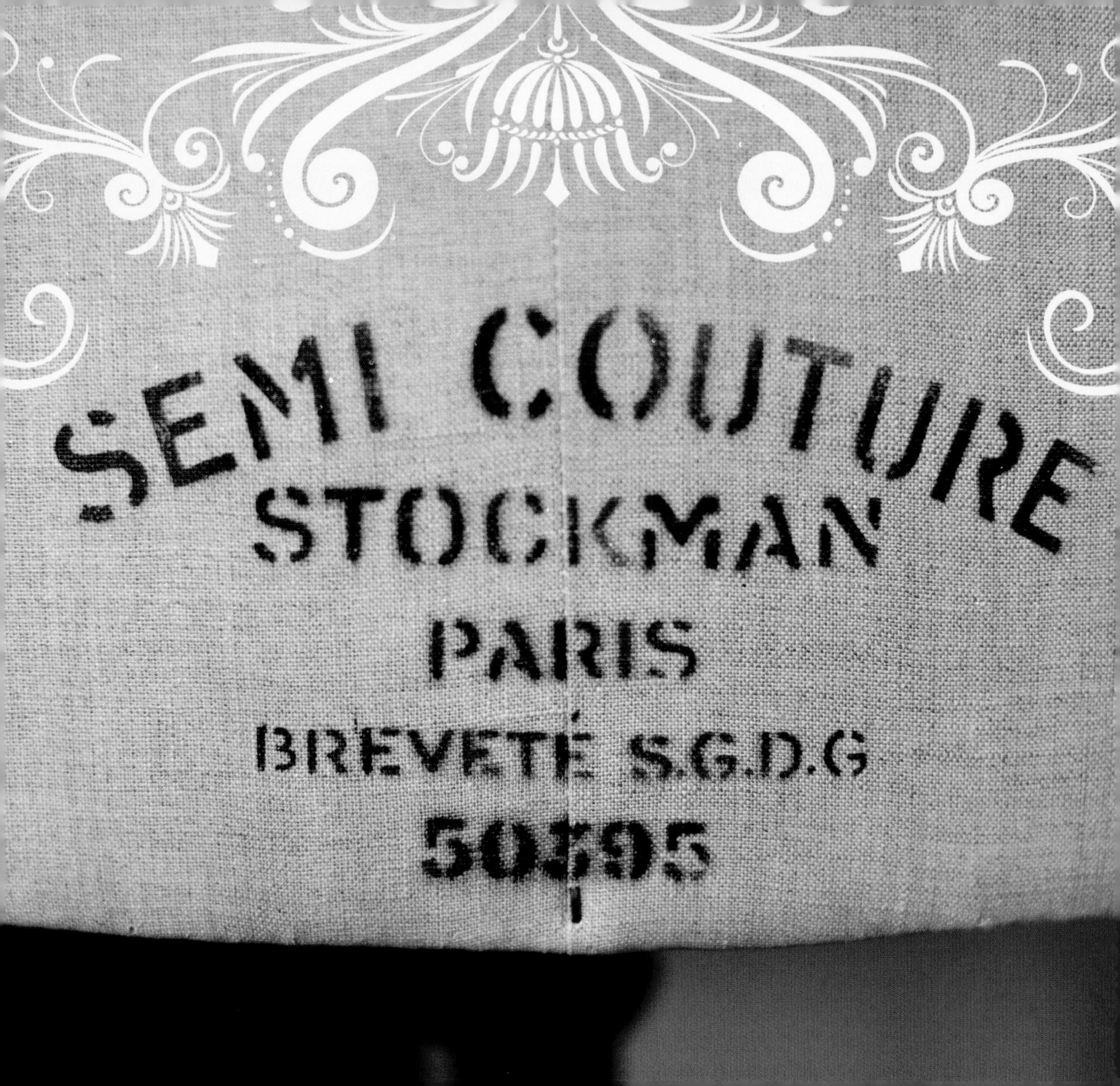
SEMI COUTURE
STOCKMAN
PARIS
BREVETÉ S.G.D.G
50395

Fashion Guides

We couldn't possibly include all of the fabulous shopping boutiques in this guide, so if your appetite has been whetted and you want more, more, MORE, then get some expert advice and pack an up-to-date shopping guide such as the fabulous *A Shopper's Guide to Paris Fashion* by Alicia Drake, *Where to Wear Paris* by Jill Fairchild and Gerri Gallagher, or *Best Buys to French Chic* by Rachel Kaplan. For the absolute latest word on *la mode Parisienne*, head to the **Librairie de la Mode** (22 rue Pierre-Lescot, 1st, tel 01 40 13 81 50), a boutique specializing in international fashion and design magazines.

Does it Really Matter How I Look?

Of course! As a visitor to a foreign city, your primary form of communication will be unspoken. You probably won't be able to show off your sparkling wit, university degrees, or flair at entertaining, but you can make a lasting impression with the way you dress and carry yourself. Remember, it may be your only chance of making any impression at all! And if there was ever a place where people are acutely aware of not only how they look, but how everyone else looks, it's Paris. Whether it's in a chic shopping district, an elegant restaurant, or a ballet at the opera, Parisians dress up. They know that they are as much a part of the "scenery" as the beautiful settings. Enjoy the chance to be a part of this silent show!

PART IV

Get in the Mood

SEXY CULTURE

> *"Sex is a big question mark. It is something people will talk about forever."* — CATHERINE DENEUVE

Feeling sexy? Check. Looking sexy? Double check. Ready to embark on your naughty Paris adventures? Relax. We ladies never rush into anything without getting warmed up, *n'est-ce pas?*

Even when the French aren't making love, their culture keeps the sexual embers glowing by celebrating its passionate embraces, sultry seductions and illicit thrills throughout the arts and literature. Ignite your own inner fires with this provocative inspiration, from the erotic *chefs d'oeuvres* in the Louvre to the smoldering gazes of a Catherine Deneuve film. Allow the naughty boutiques of Paris to spark your wildest fantasies, whether you're "just looking" or in the market for a few racy souvenirs.

And if you're still feeling more like a wall*fleur* than a sexy siren, entrust the local experts to teach you all the right moves to awaken your body and engage your sexual prowess.

Your Naughty Paris Library

Before you can embrace your inner *femme fatale*, you need to recognize her. Rather than the homogenous images found in fashion magazines, look to the unforgettable heroines of literature — French literature, *bien sûr* — for inspiration. After all, every self-respecting Parisian woman is a well-read woman. And if you can't return to Paris as often as you'd like, a home library well-stocked with French classics is an indulgent diversion that you can return to again and again and again.

Five Must-Read Sexy Novels

With so *many* juicy French novels to choose from, where do you start? These recommendations by Helena Frith-Powell, author of *Two Lipsticks and a Lover*, are a great place to jumpstart your intellectual stimulation.

Chéri by Colette (1920)

A very sensual book, Chéri is the story of an older woman being perused by a much younger man, "an idea which we Anglophones don't accept as readily as the French," says Helena. "And he's simply beautiful, married to a young wife, but the older woman still has the upper hand, which is very sexy." Colette remains a role model for many French women, dancing on tables at the Ritz well into her 60s and marrying her son-in-law. "She was very naughty."

Les Liaisons Dangereuses by Choderlos de Laclos (1782)

This is a classic tale of two aristocrats who turn the game of seduction into an art form, using whatever deceitful means necessary to get what they want. "It's the perfect combination of politesse and raw lust, every emotion is governed by sensuality, sexuality, and social restraints," explains Helena. "It's how the French see the world."

Bonjour Tristesse by Françoise Sagan (1954)
If a novel can't be set in Paris, the French Riviera is the next best place. The sea and the sun create the backdrop for this very French coming-of-age story of 17-year-old Cécile and the lessons of her womanizing father, Raymond. This "sexy, poignant, moving and brief book" was written by the author when she was just 18.

Madame Bovary by Gustave Flaubert (1856)
Attacked for obscenity when it was first published, this novel reads like a 19th-century version of Bridget Jones. Although we wouldn't want to emulate the unfortunate Emma's destructive love affairs and subsequent suicide, Flaubert's skillful writing evokes some deliciously erotic scenes. Madame Bovary regularly tops international lists as one of the greatest books of all time.

The Delta of Venus by Anaïs Nin (1978)
Nin was a daring French woman who made a name for herself as one of the first prominent writers of female erotica. This collection of erotic short stories, written in the 1940s and published posthumously, is considered one of her best books.

A Naughty tip

Look for bilingual editions of the classics so that you can instantly learn the French version of your favorite lines.

Your French Film Fix

Sometimes a lady needs more than a good book to satisfy her cravings. Lose yourself in the sights and sounds of these sexy flicks, some French, all filmed in France.

Sabrina (1954, American) Forget the remake. Audrey Hepburn as Sabrina made us all fall in love with Paris when she says to Linus (Humphrey Bogart): "Paris isn't for changing planes, it's for changing your outlook! For throwing open the windows and letting in... letting in la vie en rose!"

Jules et Jim (1962, French) Truffaut's New Wave classic is a *ménage-à-trois* story of two friends, Jules and Jim, who tragically fall for the same woman, Catherine (played by Jeanne Moreau). "She's every French man's fantasy," says Helena. "It's just a very sexy film."

Belle de Jour (1967, French) French film siren Catherine Deneuve stars as the original desperate housewife who spends her afternoons working in a brothel to fulfill her sexual fantasies.

Last Tango in Paris (1973, American) A young and strapping Marlon Brando dives head first into a sadistic affair with a French woman while mourning the death of his wife. You'll never look at butter the same way again.

Henry & June (1990, American) Novelist Henry Miller (Fred Ward) and his actress wife June (played by Uma Thurman) become entwined in the Bohemian lifestyle of 1930s Paris with their friend and benefactor Anaïs Nin.

La Reine Margot (1994, French) A passionate, violent, and riveting period film about Henri IV's first wife, Margaret de Valois (Isabelle Adjani). Henri is played well by Daniel Auteuil, but it's the steamy scenes with Margaret's lover La Môle (the exquisite Vincent Perez) that will really get your attention.

L'Appartement (1996, French) Vincent Cassel and Monica Bellucci got married three years after starring in this Hitchcock-style tale of passion and voyeurism. This is why French men follow beautiful women through the streets...

Le Libertin (2000, French) A fun and raunchy period film about vice and virtue, set in a country chateau just before the French Revolution. The French may scoff at the historical accuracy, but Vincent Perez's full-frontal and the naughty antics of Audrey Tautou and Arielle Dombasle make it a must-see.

Moulin Rouge (2001, Australian/American) Baz Luhrmann's contemporary take on France's famous cabaret is an indulgent feast for the eyes and ears. Who cares if Nicole Kidman and Ewan McGregor's passion seems forced? You'll melt to the tango rendition of Police's "Roxanne."

Chocolat (2001, British/American) This film has everything we ladies adore: a strong and independent single mother (Juliette Binoche), a decadent chocolate shop in a little French village, and her dangerously sexy gypsy lover, played by the divine Johnny Depp. Sigh...

Naughty Masterpieces

Allow yourself be shamelessly seduced by the great masters of the art world. No one back home will raise an eyebrow if you tell them you spent your Parisian *séjour* admiring the fine *chefs d'oeuvres* of the city's renowned museums. Ah, but if only they knew. Adds a whole new meaning to the phrase, "get cultured," *non*?

MUSÉE DU QUAI BRANLY

37 QUAI BRANLY, 7TH.
TEL 01 56 61 70 00
RER PONT ALMA
OPEN 10 A.M. - 6:30 P.M., THURSDAY UNTIL 9:30 P.M.
CLOSED MONDAY.
WWW.QUAIBRANLY.FR

This sleek and seductive Primitive Arts museum is open late on Thursday nights. Forget about square rooms and white walls; here you'll weave your way through undulating, leather-clad barriers to darkened galleries where visitors circle spot-lit displays in glass cases...you can pretend you're looking at the art instead of the handsome stranger on the other side. Finish with a late meal upstairs at Les Ombres (see **After Dark Rendez-Vous**), with a view of the sparkling Iron Lady.

MUSÉE D'ORSAY

1 RUE LÉGION D'HONNEUR (QUAI ANATOLE FRANCE), 7TH.
M° SOLFERINO OR RER C MUSÉE D ORSAY
TEL 01 40 49 48 14
OPEN 9:30 A.M.-6 P.M. (THURSDAYS UNTIL 9:45 P.M.).
CLOSED MONDAY.
WWW.MUSEE-ORSAY.FR

There's something inherently dramatic, even arousing, about train stations. You may not be boarding the *Orient Express* for Venice, but you can still enjoy the fascinating (painted) landscapes while strolling in this former Art Nouveau station. Since 1986 it has housed a collection of art from the period of 1848-1914, when some of the biggest scandals in the art world took place, such as Auguste Clésinger's erotic sculpture, *Femme Piquée par un Serpent*. Sure, the Impressionists seem harmless now, but the bold gaze of Manet's *Olympia* still stops men in their tracks (stand aside and watch if you doubt it), and few will be able to find words when faced with the notorious tribute to the female genitalia in Courbet's *Origine du Monde*. Spot a fine specimen among your fellow museum-goers? Enjoy a bit of mischievous cat-and-mouse surveillance from the Orsay's open mezzanines...

MUSÉE DE L'EROTISME

78, BOULEVARD DE CLICHY, 18TH.
Mº PIGALLE OR BLANCHE
TEL 01 42 58 28 73
OPEN DAILY 10 A.M. - 2 A.M.
WWW.MUSEE-EROTISME.COM

It's just past midnight and you and your companion are strolling the neon-lit streets of Pigalle. Maybe you just finished a romantic meal in Montmartre, or a show at the Moulin Rouge. But no one would ever be so indiscreet as to ask what you're doing in the city's infamous red-light district. Rest assured that it's safe, if not pretty. And look here, there's even a museum, open late to accommodate all of the midnight wanderers out looking for a cultural nightcap before heading back to the privacy of their own *boudoir*.

Spread out over several floors, the Erotica Museum titillates with artworks and objects from the five continents and spanning several centuries. The collection of Belle Epoch brothel photos is particularly fascinating, while the contemporary exhibitions might evoke a slightly more disturbed reaction. But really, you wouldn't be a lady if you didn't find *something* shocking within these five floors.

A Note for Solo Ladies

Pigalle on your own is best visited during daylight hours to avoid any discomfort. You can always claim you're wearing sunglasses because of the unfortunate fluorescent lighting.

Extra Naughty *Become a Muse*

Dream of becoming an artist's model? Look for bulletin board ads (or post your own) around art schools such as the Académie de la Grande Chaumière (14 rue de la Grande Chaumière, 6th), art supply stores like Sennelier (3 quai Voltaire, 6th), the Anglophone magazine FUSAC (found in all English-language book stores in Paris) or online (Craig's List Paris). Need a little inspiration? There's an erotic novel about an American woman who becomes an artist's model in Paris called, coincidentally…Naughty Paris (by Jina Bacarr). No relation to this guidebook, but can you ever have too many books titled "Naughty Paris" in your library?

MUSÉE RODIN
79, RUE DE VARENNE, 7TH.
TEL 01 44 18 61 10
Mº VARENNE
OPEN 9:30 A.M.-5:45 P.M. (4:45 P.M. IN WINTER). CLOSED MONDAY.
WWW.MUSEE-RODIN.FR

PETIT PALAIS
AVENUE WINSTON CHURCHILL, 8TH.
TEL 01 53 43 40 00
Mº CHAMPS-ELYSÉES-CLÉMENCEAU
OPEN 10 A.M. - 6 P.M. CLOSED MONDAY.
WWW.PETITPALAIS.PARIS.FR

See Rodin's innocently provocative statues such as *The Kiss*, as well as the artist's vast, yet lesser-known collection of erotic drawings (you'll find a copy of "Rodin, les Figures d'Eros" at the museum book store). And the gardens are full of hidden corners to protect the public eyes from any overt displays of affection...

A jewel box of fine arts masterpieces, this elegant municipal museum seems like such a *nice* place to take the family. But the naughty curators made sure that no one would miss Clesinger's writhing marble *Bacchante*, placed directly in the center of the main gallery, nor the suggestively entwined ladies of Courbet's painting *Le Sommeil*.

MUSÉE DU LOUVRE

99 RUE DE RIVOLI, 1ST.
M° PALAIS-ROYAL-MUSÉE-DU-LOUVRE OR LOUVRE-RIVOLI
TEL 01 40 20 53 17
OPEN 9 A.M. - 6 P.M., WEDNESDAY AND FRIDAY UNTIL 9:45 P.M.
CLOSED TUESDAY.
WWW.LOUVRE.FR

Break away from the herds of tourists heading *en masse* to see the Louvre triumvirate (Mona Lisa, Winged Victory, Venus de Milo) and slip into the less crowded galleries housing some of the museum's erotic masterpieces by French painters such as Ingres' *Grande Odalisque*, Girodet's *Sleep of Endymion*, or James Pradier's *Satyre et Bacchante* in marble. **Note**: The Satyr is said to resemble the face of the artist, and the Bacchante the face of his mistress, the actress Juliette Drouot. Pradier's own wife was, herself, seeing the writer Gustave Flaubert, and supposedly became his inspiration for *Madame Bovary*.

Naughty Tip: If it's Wednesday or Friday, have a Happy Hour apéritif at Le Fumoir (see **After Dark Rendez-Vous**). By 8 p.m. the Louvre's low-lit galleries will be almost devoid of frazzled families and tour groups, making it the perfect time for a bit of leisurely art admiration à deux. What better way to whet your appetite?

"When it comes to French films, you need to abandon all rationality and just abandon yourself to the senses. You don't always understand what's going on, but that's very French."

—*HELENA FRITH-POWELL*

Alfresco inspiration

- **Cimetière Père-Lachaise** (Boulevard de Ménilmontant, 20th): Not only does this hillside cemetery have an amazing collection of funerary statues, some of them are downright risqué. The bronze statue of the young Victor Noir has become a good luck symbol of fertility for women who take a shine to the suggestive bulge below the belt, and the winged sphinx crowning the grave of the naughty Irish scribe Oscar Wilde (relieved of its manhood by vandals) is perpetually smothered in lipstick smooches.

- **Jardin du Luxembourg** (Rue de Médicis & Boulevard St-Michel, 6th): Queen Marie de Médici, the scheming widow of Henri IV, never got to appreciate her beautiful gardens and Florentine palace before her banishment. She might have been thinking of her illicit lover when commissioning the provocative Médici Fountain. Today's lovers seek refuge from the outside world in the winding alleys of the garden's west end, dotted with sculptures of Chopin, Baudelaire, Delacroix…and even a small Statue of Liberty.

Naughty Tours

While you may picture yourself gliding gracefully through the museums of Paris overcome with admiration for all of the beautiful works of art, the reality is not always so glamorous. Enlist a private guide to whisk you past the lines, ensure that you never need to glance at a map in the endless galleries, and bring alive even the most puzzling masterpieces. And lest you think you're the only one interested in the naughty paintings and erotic sculptures, here are two guides specializing in artistic bosoms, marble backsides, and illicit *baisers*.

Naughty Tip
Just Looking? Please, do!

Paris is a city of lovers who feel no need to hide their public displays of affection. Be captivated by the sight of them entwined on the bridge, seductive glances between strangers in the metro, flirtatious exchanges on café terraces...no need to avert your eyes. They know you're watching. And they're watching you, too. It's all part of the visual feast that makes Paris so intoxicating. Does the very idea make you blush? Remember, you can always look away. But no telling what you'd be missing...

JEAN-MANUEL TRAIMOND

TEL 01 47 37 42 70 OR 06 86 10 57 33
E-MAIL: HLBHLB@HOTMAIL.COM

Jean-Manuel is a lively French gentleman whose knowledge about erotic art is matched only by his enthusiasm for sharing it in his impeccable English (Danish, too). Tours are available in the Louvre, Musée d'Orsay, and even the Musée de l'Erotisme, "although so far no one has requested this." He also does tours of Parisian gardens, which are simply bursting with suggestive statues.

Note: If you can't have Jean-Manuel in person, pick up a copy of his book, the illustrated *Guide Erotique du Louvre et Musée D'Orsay*, available in French or Italian at the museum bookshops.

BRUNO DE BAECQUE

TEL 01 42 01 37 16 OR 06 82 29 37 44
WWW.VUSOUSCETANGLE.NET

Bruno is a typical French intellectual with atypical views on art. He leads as a series of art tours called "Vu sous cet Angle" (*Seen under this Angle*), including naughty tours of the Louvre and the Musée d'Orsay (for adults only).

Naughty Shopping

Art & Literature

For ladies who prefer to keep their gaze averted in public, here is a careful selection of addresses where you can purchase erotic books and artworks to enjoy in privacy, *chez vous.*

GALERIE AU BONHEUR DU JOUR

11 RUE CHABANAIS, 2ND.
TEL 01 42 96 58 64
M° PYRAMIDES
WWW.AUBONHEURDUJOUR.NET

A quiet side street between the Palais Royal and Opéra Garnier, an elegant corner façade…ring the bell and the owner will welcome you inside her bright and modern gallery. A stylish woman "of a certain age" as they say in France, Nicole Canet has a unique collection of vintage and modern erotic photography. The first two rooms present the latest themed exhibitions, such as Exotic Beauties, Sailors & Legionnaires, Corsets & Lace, and Early Cinema Stars. Whether male or female, clothed or nude, vintage or modern, the images are chosen for their erotic and artistic sensuality. Browse the boxes of matted silver gelatin prints and then ask Nicole to show you the Boudoir, a darker room with deep red walls where Nicole presents erotic paintings, engravings, rare books, and *objets d'art* such as naughty statues and even an antique chastity belt. Can you think of a better souvenir of your naughty Paris adventure than an original erotic photograph in impeccable condition? "Women never buy photographs," she says with a sigh. A challenge, ladies?

Naughty Aside

If the name of the street rings a bell, you may already have read about the city's infamous bordellos known as *maisons closes*, legal until 1946. The most luxurious among them was Le Chabanais (located across the street at #12), where princes, politicians, and the rich and famous from around the world would come for Champagne baths and high-class entertainment with the most beautiful women in town. Today the nondescript façade reveals nothing of its illustrious past, but you might be able to guess who can show you a limited edition portfolio of photos taken during the bordello's prime…

LA MUSARDINE

122 RUE CHEMIN VERT, 11TH.
TEL 01 49 29 48 55
M° PÈRE-LACHAISE
WWW.LAMUSARDINE.COM

TASCHEN

2 RUE DE BUCI, 6TH.
TEL 01 40 51 79 22
M° ODÉON
WWW.TASCHEN.COM

You can enter this bookstore without having to hide your face. Bright and friendly, this shop is frequented by perfectly normal looking clientele browsing the oversized art books, flipping through graphic novels, and perusing the discreet DVD selection. Musardine is also a publisher, and their annual guide, *Paris Sexy*, is the number one source in print for knowing every corner of Paris dedicated to sex (primarily for men, but also gay, lesbian, women). More light-hearted and sure to bring a smile to your face are the *Osez* guides to sex ("Oser" means "To Dare"), illustrated with amusing cartoons that bring the fun back into sex, daring readers to learn everything from swinging and oral sex to nudist vacations and how to rev up your honeymoon night. If your French is limited, try the erotic art books, or, if they're not already sold out, the annual *Dieux des Stades* (Gods of the Stadiums) calendar featuring nude French athletes in all their masculine glory.

You can pretend you wandered into this sexy little bookshop to look at the beautiful books on art, architecture, pop culture, design, or fashion…but everyone knows that these innocent books simply made it easier for Taschen to discreetly usher their erotic art books into mainstream consciousness. If a titillating art book sits on your home coffee table, chances are it's from Taschen. So it's no surprise that their Paris boutique, designed by the beloved French interior architect Philippe Starck, is also a stylish work of art. Come after dark when the low-lit aisles, lined with dark wood flooring and bronze-plated shelves, take on the atmosphere of a trendy bar. Lock eyes over a limited edition Helmut Newton book. Graze his sleeve when reaching for the last hand-made photo book of erotica produced by Chez Higgins. By the time the doors close at midnight, you should have at least one decent candidate to join you for a drink at Le Bar.

I think anything that has to do with sexuality makes people very interested.
—CATHERINE DENEUVE

LES LARMES D'ÉROS

58 RUE AMELOT, 11TH.
TEL 01 43 38 33 43
M° ST-SÉBASTIEN-FROISSART
WWW.EROSCONNEXION.COM

There's something fascinating about vintage guide books to Paris; even better if it's a naughty guide. Jocelyn and Alexandre's discreet little boutique, a short walk from the Place de la Bastille, specializes in erotic photography and art books, some which they publish themselves. But the real pleasure here is finding unexpected treasures hiding among the stacks of vintage erotica and boxes of rare books and old photographs, like the bilingual 1950s guidebook, "Comment et où s'amuser à Paris" (*How and Where to Enjoy Oneself in Paris*). For adult reading only, *bien sûr...*

UN REGARD MODERNE

10 RUE GÎT-LE-COEUR, 6TH.
TEL 01 43 29 13 93
M° ST-MICHEL

Tiny, tiny boutique off Place St-Michel, packed floor-to-ceiling with erotic literature, pornographic comics, and an eclectic selection of counter-culture paperbacks. Many rare books and limited editions hidden among the stacks. Put on your best damsel in distress expression if you want to find something specific.

CHEZ HIGGINS EDITIONS

5, RUE DE L'ANCIENNE COMÉDIE, 6TH.
TEL 01 43 54 28 84
Mº ODÉON
WWW.CHEZHIGGINS.COM

The showroom and "curiosity cabinet" of this exclusive publisher is only open by prior *rendez-vous*. And it's worth the effort. Take your time choosing among the beautifully hand-crafted, limited edition, erotic photo books, each one more exquisite than the last. A unique gift for someone special...why not you, *chérie*?

A dirty book is rarely dusty. – ANONYMOUS

LA ROSE NOIRE

67 RUE CONDORCET, 9TH.
TEL 01 40 16 02 70
Mº ANVERS

A small shop featuring new and vintage erotic books and graphic novels, all catalogued for easy referencing. Located near the up-and-coming hipster hangout, Rue des Martyrs.

IMAGES DE DEMAIN

141 RUE SAINT MARTIN, 4TH.
TEL 01 44 54 99 99
Mº RAMBUTEAU

This poster shop across from the Pompidou Centre is the perfect place to pick up a few inexpensive postcards...erotic black and white vintage photos, saucy Parisian ladies, cabaret and Belle Epoch paintings, and many other famously naughty images by Man Ray, Brassaï, and Toulouse-Lautrec. Fill out your postcards with news of your own Paris adventures while sipping espresso in the adorable second floor tearoom.

Don't Forget
Yoba, Nuits Blanches and the Dollhouse also carry a selection of saucy books targeted especially for ladies (see Toys for Madame).

Toys for Madame

It's not the size of the equipment… and we're not just talking about French "ticklers". The Parisians may not have been the first to open up ladies-only toy boutiques, but they do it with such *panache* it's easy to forgive them. And yes, you can get most of this stuff back home, but there's just something naughtier about saying to the airport security agents, nonchalantly, "Oh, I got that in Paris…."

Fun and Kitsch

Cutesy, non-threatening toy boutiques are now popping up all over Paris, many with the same products imported from the US, UK, and Germany including the Rabbit, the Kama Sutra line of body products, and the now ubiquitous Rub My Duckie. Pick up your kitsch gifts here (such as "I Love Paris" condom magnets). Both are just around the corner from the Pompidou Centre at Châtelet: 1969 Paris (5 rue des Lombards, 4th, tel 01 48 04 03 30. www.1969.fr) and Passage du Désir (aka the Love Store, 11 rue St-Martin, 4th, tel 09 54 65 12 34 www.passagedudesir.fr).

SONIA RYKIEL WOMAN

6 RUE DE GRENELLE, 6TH.
TEL 01 49 54 66 21
M° ST-SULPICE
WWW.SONIARYKIEL.FR

LES NUITS BLANCHES

16 RUE DE TOURNELLES, 4TH
TEL 01 42 77 60 51
M° BASTILLE
WWW.ARTISTICVIBRATION.COM

Sex is one of the nine reasons for reincarnation. The other eight are unimportant.
— HENRY MILLER

It all started here, in the basement of this famous Parisian *prêt-à-porter* boutique. Nathalie Rykiel, who designs alongside her mother Sonia, created the first chic and "female-friendly" place where Parisian ladies could buy their intimate massage products in style. Adults only are allowed downstairs, accompanied by a knowledgeable hostess who will kindly explain the pro's and con's of each and every *objet érotique.*

Sleek and elegant, this designer boutique looks more like a contemporary art gallery than a sex toy shop. No mere coincidence. Anna, the charming Italian owner, has chosen only the most unique and precious *objets d'art* for her boutique. Hand-blown glass dildos "Made in France," sexy jewelry, and latex lingerie are displayed like artworks alongside a collection of the best erotic guides and naughty literature in English and French. Ask Anna to put you on the mailing list for invitations to the art exhibitions and product launch parties.

Naughty resource

The French magazine S'Toys (www.stoys.fr) combines fashion, beauty, and…sex toy reviews. At French newsstands every two months.

AMOURS, DÉLICES ET ORGUES

4 RUE DE LA CORDERIE, 3RD.
TEL 01 44 54 98 62
M° TEMPLE OR RÉPUBLIQUE
WWW.AMOURSDELICESETORGUES.COM

Overlooking a leafy square in the increasingly trendy northern Marais district, this very feminine boutique of "loves, delights and…organs" is full of pretty pink and purple accessories, racy lingerie, scented candles, gifts for lovers, and, in the back room, the aforementioned "organs" in Pyrex glass, silicon rubber and latex.

DOLLHOUSE

24 RUE ROI DE SICILE, 4TH.
TEL 01 40 27 09 21
M° ST-PAUL
WWW.JEUXDEFILLES.FR

Caroline and Delphine welcome ladies (and their well-behaved gentlemen) into their fun and colorful Marais district boutique. Upstairs is devoted to sexy lingerie, while downstairs are the erotic games, *risqué* restraints, naughty toys and pillows with hidden compartments to hide them. They have a lovely collection of matching handcuff and mask sets, and custom-made whips, crops, and floggers. Regular erotic art exhibitions decorate the walls.

Don't Forget

Yoba *(see Oh là là Lingerie)* has a fine collection of very elegant and refined toys for the boudoir, as well as their own line of sensual bath and body products. For a more hardcore collection of naughty playthings, it's hard to beat **Démonia** *(see Latex, Leather & Fetish)*.

Naughty Tip

The art of tying a scarf…make sure it's firmly knotted, but not too tight, nor tied in a slip knot. If your man is smart he's not going to try to escape, so gentle but firm restraint is all that's necessary. And for fashion's sake, keep the Hermès scarves safely tucked away. While a sinfully smooth silk blindfold may heighten the senses, it will be your dry-cleaning bill that will be heightened later when the mascara smudges won't come off. PS: If you were looking for tips on how to tie a French scarf around your neck, you're reading the wrong book, darling.

Latex, Leather & Fetish

Whether you're getting equipped for a Paris fetish soirée or your own private boudoir fantasy reen-actment, nothing brings out your sexy alter ego like a fabulously naughty wardrobe. Go wild with the feather boas, stiletto boots, and leather corsets…or pick up that perfect little French maid costume.

Extra Naughty

Want to turn up the heat on a chilly day of Parisian sightseeing? Slip the remote control of your vibrating toy into your man's hand and tell him you're going to test the range…for research purposes, of course.

MÉTAMORPH'OSE

49 RUE QUINCAMPOIX, 4TH.
TEL 01 42 72 21 98
M° CHÂTELET
WWW.METAMORPHOSE.FR

Far from the seedy red-light district, this prêt à oser ("ready to dare") boutique is just around the corner from the Pompidou Centre. Don't let the small entrance fool you. Madame will lead you downstairs, where you'll find room after room of costumes, corsets, shoes, leather gloves, vinyl bustiers, rubber dresses, bondage accessories and sexy toys. It could take all day to choose something in this Ali Baba's cavern.

PHYLEA

61 RUE QUINCAMPOIX, 4TH.
TEL 01 42 76 01 80
M° CHÂTELET

Ladies with a taste for the theatrical will find it hard to pass by the windows of this colorful boutique without stepping inside. Imagine a flamboyant wardrobe filled with one-of-a-kind corsets in every style and fabric—feathers and leather, silk and brocade, rubber and velvet—many with matching ankle-length skirts for a more formal look. There are also waist cinchers, rubber, leather and PVC wear, sexy dresses, lingerie, and even a super-sexy French maid costume, *oh là là!* In the back are more traditional S&M accessories, high heels, restraints, and masks.

BOUTIQUE DÉMONIA

22 AVENUE JEAN AICARD, 11TH.
TEL 01 43 14 82 70
M° MÉNILMONTANT
WWW.DEMONIA.COM

Aesthetically, Démonia could use a woman's touch.
But this old school sex shop with the bright fluorescent
lighting and generic metal racks is the veritable HQ for
the city's fetish/S&M community. Come here first to
find flyers and pre-purchase tickets for upcoming events
and parties (*soirées*), including the annual Nuit Démonia,
a fetish party that attracts aficionados from around the
world. Discreetly located on a cobblestoned street across
from a small park (look for the red door with the black
"D"), the shop carries a hard-core assortment of leather,
latex, and PVC clothing, costumes, and *très* naughty toys.

REBECCA RILS

76-78 BOULEVARD DE CLICHY, 18TH.
TEL 01 46 71 84 13
WWW.REBECCARILS.COM

There are few places a lady would want to venture
alone in the Pigalle red-light district, more out
of distaste than actual danger. But this friendly
Supermarché Érotique (yes, there are even shopping
carts) next to the Musée de l'Érotisme and Moulin
Rouge successfully woos 30-something Parisian
women and young couples into its vast temple of
erotic lingerie, fetishwear, sex toys, wigs and f**k-
me-pumps made to be worn in bed. Also a selection
of "only the most tasteful" pornographic DVDs. Open
until midnight.

Get Disguised: Costumes

You never know when the occasion will arise…a costumed ball? Are you going to be a 17th-century marquise? A
Second Empire princess? An Oriental dancer? A Venetian noble? Before boarding the Orient Express to Venice,
find the perfect costume at Sommier (3 Passage Brady, 10th, tel 01 42 08 27 01, www.sommier.com) specialists
in costume rentals since 1922. Another fascinating address for masks, capes, wigs and feathers is Theatr'Hall (3
Carrefour de l'Odéon, 6th, tel 08 71 74 00 36, www.theatrhall.net), a boutique specializing in high-quality men's
theatre costumes and period wear. Want to know if blondes have more fun? Find ladies' wigs at Rebecca Rils.

SENSUAL EDUCATION

French is the undisputed language of love...

Learn the Right Moves

Y ou've read the books, studied the guides, and maybe even experimented on your own *chez vous*. But nothing can compare to the hands-on *savoir-faire* offered by these experts for a sexy boost of confidence.

PLEASURE COACHING
DIVINE FEMININE TOUCH WITH VICTORIA STRONG
WWW.DIVINEFEMININETOUCH.COM

Just being in Paris doesn't always guarantee that its undercurrent of erotic *mojo* will seep into your body through osmosis. Sometimes it helps to have a gentle nudge in the right direction to get in touch with your inner *femme fatale*. American-born pleasure coach Victoria Strong is the expert on sexual wellbeing and erotic empowerment for women, men and couples. Whether your sleepy libido needs a kick-start, or you simply want to learn a few new tricks to drive your partner wild, her innovative body-based pleasure coaching can help you discover hidden erogenous zones, overcome sexual blocks, and learn new skills to heighten your own desire.

Eroticism is one of the basic means of self-knowledge, as indispensable as poetry. —ANAÏS NIN

Victoria is an attentive listener who immediately puts clients at ease in her safe and welcoming central-Paris studio. Custom-tailored pleasure coaching and sensual bodywork sessions from €175.

POLE DANCING
PINK SCHOOL AT PINK PARADISE
49 RUE PONTHIEU, 8TH.
TEL 01 58 36 19 20
M° CHAMPS-ELYSÉES-CLEMENCEAU
WWW.PINKPARADISE.FR

Your local gym back home may offer pole dancing classes, but that just takes all of the naughtiness out of it. In Paris, the best place to learn how to swing sexily around a pole is at the Pink Paradise Gentleman's Club. Their Pink School offers beginner and advanced classes in "Pole Dancing and Seduction," from €25. Essential school supplies: a pair of short shorts and your highest heels. The instructors are French, but you'll be learning by seeing and doing, not reading a text book.

STRIPTEASE

ARTSTRIP
WWW.ARTSTRIP-WORLD.COM

Dying to perform a sexy striptease for your man,
but terrified of looking silly or tripping on your
panties? Put yourself in the expert hands of ArtStrip
instructor Violeta, who will teach you the secret
moves and techniques to transform you into a pro in
no time. For even more fun, book a private class for
you and your friends in your hotel (from €80).

Note: Don't worry, no bare naked ladies here!
You'll practice wearing two sets of lingerie (one to
take off, one to leave on). English spoken.

Don't tell a woman she's pretty; tell her there's
no other woman like her, and all roads will
open to you.

—WRITER *JULES RENARD*

The French Tongue

French is the undisputed language of love, and *les Français* have no shortage of terms associated with making *l'amour*, including the infamously naughty *ménage-à-trois* and *Voulez-vous coucher avec moi (ce soir)?* You'll have no trouble finding a willing Frenchman to help you hone your seductive language skills. Just be sure you know when to replace those sweet nothings with discreet refusals.

Note: The French are great admirers of les bons mots, but don't spend too much of your precious time in Paris stressing over the mot juste. The language of love isn't always a verbal one. And a subtle smile, a non-committal shrug, or a withering glare can get you just as far as any advanced grammatical abilities.

Making Contact

It's always a good idea to find out where you stand right away, so go ahead and ask, **Do you speak English?** *Parlez-vous anglais?(par-lay-voo' ahn-glay')*. If they start rambling off incomprehensibly, you should be flattered that they think you're fluent, but it will eventually be time to **confess that you don't speak French**: *Excusez-moi, je ne parle pas français (ex-koo'-say-mwa, zhuh ne parl pa' frahn-say')*, or simply explain that **you don't understand:** *Je ne comprends pas (zhuh ne com'-prond pa')*.

Pick-up Lines

If you get caught making eyes, *Monsieur* may use the old line, **Do we know each other?** *On se connait? (on se con-ay')*, or **offer to buy you a drink**: *Je vous offre un verre? (zhuh voos off'-ruh un vair')* As soon as he hears your accent, he will most likely **ask where you're from:** *Vous venez d'où? (voo ven'-ay doo')*, although if your French is shaky or non-existent he will hopefully switch over to English at this point. If you're feeling bold enough to make the first contact yourself, keep it simple with a classic **hello/good evening**: *Bonjour/Bonsoir (bon-zhor'/bon-swar')*, perhaps adding a casual **How's it going?** *Ca va?* (*sa-va'*) or **Are you having a nice evening?** *Vous passez une bonne soirée (voo pass-ay' oon bon swar-ay')?*

Madame or Mademoiselle?

Historically, the title Mademoiselle referred to girls and single women. Only marriage could bestow ladies with the title of Madame. Today it's more commonly used for any woman once she reaches adulthood, whether married or not —— an admittedly subjective viewpoint. You can gently correct any suitors who call you mademoiselle, but it will still leave them wondering whether you're married or simply wish to be taken more seriously.

For Clarity

Not that it will put a stop to the average Frenchman's seduction plans, but you may feel inclined to **say you're married**, *Je suis mariée (zhuh swee' marry-ay')*, **engaged** *Je suis fiancée (zhuh swee' fee-ahn-say')*, or that **you have a boyfriend** *J'ai un copain (zhay' un co-pan')*. If your suitor appears as soon as your companion leaves your side, you can inform him that **he is your lover**, *C'est mon amant (say mon ah-maw')*, or **just a friend:** *C'est juste un ami (say zhoost' un ah-mee')*. Your intentions may become more clear if you **declare that you're single** *Je suis célibataire(zhuh swee' sel-leeb'-uh-tair')*. He may not volunteer the information, so if it matters be sure to **ask if he has a girlfriend** *Vous avez une copine?(voos ah-vay' oon co-peen')* **or married** *Vous êtes marié? (voos ett' marry-ay')*.

Decoding His Amorous Declarations

It's not uncommon in Paris, when passing men in the street, to hear them exclaim **how charming you are**: *Vous êtes très charmante (voos ett tray' sharm-ont')*. The more daring ones may tell you **you're beautiful**: *Vous êtes belle (vooz ett bell')*. You can return the compliments with a discreet smile…or not. It will be very hard to resist smiling when you elicit your first authentic *oh là là!* **(wow!)** from a French admirer. When out on the town after dark, the men will certainly remark **how sexy you are**: *Vous êtes trop sexy! (vooz ett' tro sex-ee')*, and if your moves on the dance floor encourage one to whisper into your ear that **you are sizzling hot** *Vous êtes chaude! (vooz ett shode')*, he will typically be looking for more than just a dance partner for the evening. While most of us know that *Je t'aime (zhuh tem')* is French for **I love you**, newly acquainted lovers more typically will **declare their adoration**, *Je t'adore (zhuh ta-door')*.

When being addressed informally, vous êtes (vooz ett) is replaced with tu es (too ay). Up to you to decide whether Monsieur is being a bit too familiar or not.

Gentle Put-Downs

Unwanted attention is almost inevitable in Paris. If you're politely flattered but still want to dissuade any gentlemen, you can simply **excuse yourself** (*Excusez-moi*) and turn away. A clear **no thank you** (*Non, merci*) is sufficient when offered a drink, a seat, a dance. You can kindly try and explain that **you're waiting for someone** *J'attends quelqu'un (zhah-tond' kell-kun')*, but if Romeo still isn't getting the hint and becomes too pushy, firmly tell him to **kindly leave you alone**, *Laissez-moi tranquille, s'il vous plaît (lay'-say mwah trahn-keel', see voo play')*.

Warning!

If you hear the words salope, connasse, or pute, you're not dealing with a gentleman. You may be tempted to reply with T'es nul (You're nothing), Va te faire foutre! (Go f*** yourself), or even Casse toi! (F*** off!), however this would only make you look just as vulgar. The best response for a lady is to ignore the rude offender and briskly walk away.

Getting Naughty

Your French *beau* may (or may not) **ask permission to kiss you**: *Je peux t'embrasser? (zhuh puh' tom-brass-ay')*, but you can speed things along by **asking him to kiss you**: *Embrasse-moi! (om'-brass mwah')*. You can serenade your partner into bed with the **tongue-in-cheek formal request to sleep with you (tonight)**: *Voulez-vous coucher avec moi (ce soir)?* But serious suitors are more likely to employ the poetic **desire to make love to you**: *Je veux faire l'amour avec toi (zhuh vuh fair la-more' ah-vek twah')*. If there's still some hesitation, you (or he) could murmur a command to **get undressed**: *Déshabille-toi (days-ah'-beel twah')*.

Beware of *faux amis* or "false friends"

Confusing the noun for kiss —— un baiser —— with the verb to f**k —— baiser —— can get you in some serious linguistic trouble. So if you just want a kiss, be sure to say Embrasse-moi, not Baise-moi. To add to the confusion, the verb Faire la bise means to give air kisses (once on each cheek in Paris), and friends often say kisses! —— Bisous! (bee zoo') —— when saying goodbye.

In the Boudoir

Madame's boudoir wardrobe includes matching **bras** (*soutiens-gorges*) and **panties** (*culottes*), silky **thigh-high stockings** (*bas*) and **garter belts** (*jarretières*). Planning on stocking up on **intimate toys** (*jouets intimes*) while in Paris? The city's naughty boutiques are the perfect place to find a pair of fuzzy **handcuffs** (*menottes*), a satiny **blindfold** (*loup*), **dildos** (*godemichets* or *godes*) and **vibrators** (*vibromasseurs*) of all sizes and materials. You may even be won over by a particularly pleasing **paddle** (*tapette*) or **whip** (*martinet* or *fouet*). Learn the lingo to get the right sensation: **lace** (*dentelle*), **leather** (*cuir*), **silk** (*soie*), **PVC** (*vinyl*), **rubber** (*caoutchouc*), **glass** (*verre*) and even **stainless steel** (*acier*).

In Bed

Sex may be an international language in more ways than one—many words are similar or exactly the same in French and English: *vagin, clitoris, orgasme, masturbation, pénis, testicules, Point G, sadomasochisme, érection* and *zones érogènes*, to name a few. *Sexe anal* needs no translation, nor do the "Latin" words for *sexe oral: fellation* and *cunnilingus*. If you would like some **foreplay** (*préliminaires*), it may help to know the words for **breasts** (*seins*) and **buttocks** (*les fesses*), and the verbs **suck** (*sucer*), **lick** (*lécher*), to give a **spanking** (*donner une fessée*) and **tickle** (*chatouiller*). If you're planning on being very, very **naughty** (*coquine*), you may decide to participate in a bit of **swinging** (*échangisme* or *libertinage*) or possibly find yourself in a **threesome** (we would say *ménage à trois*, but the French actually call it *un trio*)...*oh là là*!

Naughty Note

The phrase "Pardon my French" came into use as an apology for swearing in the late 19th-century, when anything French was equated with obscenity and sex. Ironically, it's considered extremely unladylike to swear at all in France, so use les gros mots with the utmost of care.

At the Pharmacy

Feminine hygiene products (*hygiène féminine*), including **tampons** and **pads** (*tampons* and *serviettes*), are sold at pharmacies, supermarkets and most convenience stores. If you get **menstrual cramps** (*crampes menstruelles*) during your **period** (*règles*), the only place to get pain killers is at the pharmacy. A lady would never let a language barrier put her health at risk. The words for most **sexually transmitted disease**s (STD), or *Maladies Sexuellement Transmissibles (MST)* are the same; the acronym for **AIDS** is *SIDA*. *Contraception* is something you should plan for in advance if it's an issue, but in case you arrive unequipped, French pharmacies and supermarkets sell **condoms** *préservatifs* (or *capotes* in slang). The **Pill**, *La Pilule*, is only available by doctor prescription, but in cases of emergency you can get the **morning-after pill,** *contraception d'urgence* or *pilule du lendemain* from most pharmacies (some refuse to carry it) or hospitals. *Important note*: Anytime you need medicine, be sure to tell the doctor or pharmacist if you are **pregnant**, or *enceinte* (on-sant').

For women, the best aphrodisiacs are words. The G-spot is in the ears. He who looks for it below there is wasting time.

—ISABEL ALLENDE

Tip: Medical Emergency numbers and addresses can be found in the Practical Information section at the back of this guide.

In Case of Emergency
We sincerely hope you never need to use these words:

Help! *Au secours! (oh sek-or')*
Please help me *Aidez-moi, s'il vous plait (ay-day mwah', see voo play')*
I'm sick *Je suis malade (zhuh swee mal-add')*
I need a doctor *J'ai besoin d'un médecin (zhay buh-zwan' dunn med-san')*
I'm injured *Je suis blessée (zhuh swee' bless-ay')*
I need an emergency room *Aux urgences! (oze erg-onss')*
Call the police *Appelez la police (app-lay' la po-lees')*
I was attacked *J'ai été attaquée (zhay ett-ay' at-ack-ay')*
He is following me *Il me suit (eel muh swee')*
Thief *voleur or pick-pocket*
Harassment *harcèlement (har-sell-mon')*
Theft *vol*
Mugging *vol avec aggression (vole' ah-vek ag-ress-syun')*
Rape *viol (vee-ole')*

I like Frenchmen very much, because even when they insult you,
they do it so nicely. —AMERICAN ENTERTAINER *JOSEPHINE BAKER*

PART V

After Dark
Rendez-Vous

Spend your days shopping, sightseeing, and pampering yourself at the local spas, but after sunset Paris becomes the City of Light and nocturnal delights. You could easily wander into any of the popular drinking, dining or entertainment establishments of the French capital, but why play Russian roulette with your precious evening? Whether naughty or nice, these meticulously chosen venues all present a sexy setting, perfect for a night for seduction and glamour. Once you've whet your appetite at these stylish bars, intimate restaurants, sizzling dance clubs and sexy striptease shows, you may be ready for something more…daring. The second half of this chapter provides you with only the best addresses and insider advice on the city's famous sex clubs and soirées so you can choose your own naughty adventure.

Ladies of a Certain Age

In some countries, nightlife venues are virtually segregated by age group. But in Paris the generational divide is much more fluid, with men and women of all ages mixing more naturally. Even if the majority of dancers in a particular club are in their 20s, it doesn't mean ladies in their 40s aren't welcome.

WINE & DINE

Whet your appetite for seduction...

From Aperitifs to Dessert

Did someone say Champagne cocktail? *Et voilà*, an exclusive selection of the city's finest female-friendly bars for wine and spirits any time of the night, as well as restaurant bars where you can make a smooth transition from happy hour to the witching hour with an elegant meal *à table*.

Sex is as important as eating or drinking and we ought to allow the one appetite to be satisfied with as little restraint or false modesty as the other.

MARQUIS DE SADE

For the Ladies

When you're ready to meet and mingle with the local gents – either solo or with your fellow *femmes fatales* – check out these sociable Parisian bars and restaurants for an evening of flirty fun.

On Dining Solo

Most of the bars in this section also serve dinner, and are perfect for ladies dining on their own. You are never required to sit at the bar, so don't be afraid to ask for a table. When making reservations for dinner, go ahead and reserve for two, then let them know you'll be dining alone once you arrive. Tip: Doggie bags are a no-no in France, but since there are no "open container" laws, you can take that unfinished bottle of Bordeaux back to your hotel.

LE FUMOIR

6, RUE DE L'AMIRAL-COLIGNY, 1ST.
Mᵒ LOUVRE-RIVOLI
TEL 01 42 92 00 24
WWW.LEFUMOIR.FR

The art and fashion industry types who congregate here don't seem to notice the Louvre outside the large picture windows. Utterly Parisian, they may not even be aware that the antique bar was imported from a Philadelphia speakeasy. But whether alone sipping wine with a newspaper, enjoying after-work martinis with colleagues, or waiting for the *maître'd* to secure a good dinner table (preferably at the front), they're all subtly observing each other. *Et vous, Mesdames.* Cozy up with an aperitif in one of the Chesterfield sofas or test-drive your French small talk at the low-lit bar. Cocktails €10, Dinner €30-50.

KONG

1 RUE DU PONT NEUF, 1ST.
Mᵒ LOUVRE RIVOLI
TEL 01 40 39 09 00
WWW.KONG.FR

It's Happy Hour. A glass elevator ushers young executives and 30-something party girls to the contemporary bar-restaurant at the top of the Kenzo building. The food is forgettable (except for the bill), but Philippe Starck's Manga-inspired pink and Plexiglass decor and the strong cocktails appeal to this fickle fashionista crowd. Standing room only by 1 a.m., when the designer ties come off and the DJ gets the ladies dancing between the tables. You'll fit in just fine with your Vuitton Murakami bag and a mood to party. Cocktails €12, Dinner: Don't bother.

The Experimental Cocktail Club

37 RUE ST-SAUVEUR, 2ND.
Mº ETIENNE MARCEL
TEL 01 45 08 88 09
WWW.EXPERIMENTALCOCKTAILCLUB.COM

Olivier and his charming cocktail-shaking partners
have imported a bit of New York loft style into
the heart of the hip Montorgueil district. Their
minimalist-neo-baroque bar with exposed brick walls
is both sleek and cozy at the same time. Lounge on
the black leather chesterfields, or – more sociably –
at the zinc bar, where the casually stylish locals have
loosened up on the inventive Champagne and vodka
cocktails. Come with your girlfriends in the wee
hours of the weekend, or even solo if you promise
not to be a wallflower. Mingling is *de rigueur* once this
tiny bar fills up. Cocktails €9.

A Note on Drinking

Parisian ladies would never, ever allow themselves to overindulge in alcohol. "Don't get drunk, don't even think about it," says Two Lipsticks and a Lover author Helena Frith Powell. "The culture here is very different. Getting drunk is not seen as naughty, just bad behavior."

Champagne is the only wine
a woman can drink and still
remain beautiful.

—*MADAME DE POMPADOUR*

LE PIN-UP

13 RUE DE TIQUETONNE, 2ND.
M° ETIENNE-MARCEL
TEL 01 42 33 04 86
WWW.MYSPACE.COM/LEPINUP

HARRY'S NEW YORK BAR

5 RUE DAUNOU, 2ND.
M° OPÉRA
TEL 01 42 61 71 14
WWW.HARRYS-BAR.FR

Just a swizzle stick toss around the corner from the Experimental, this small bar has a surprising interior of whitewashed vaulted stone ceilings and vintage wallpaper panels. From the hanging globe lights and circular white plastic chairs to the fish-bowl-sized cocktail glasses, everything in this retro-inspired lounge recalls the voluptuous curves of the bar's namesake pin-up girls. Chill out on the mezzanine balcony overlooking the street or check out the artsy videos screened in the lower-level DJ bar. Contemporary creations such as the Cranberry Bubble (Champagne-vodka-cranberry) are mixed by the gallant Cyrille or his fabulously-coiffed co-owner Elise for their entourage of pretty young things. Champagne by the glass €6.

Rough and scruffy sexiness, just like Hemingway and his cigar-smoking barfly cronies liked it. Open since 1911, American collegiate banners still decorate the walls and downstairs is the cozy after-hours piano bar where Gershwin composed "An American in Paris." Come when you have a respectable thirst for "characters" and cocktails – the Bloody Mary and Sidecar, among others, were born here. You'll only embarrass yourself ordering soft drinks. Come late at night to play the role of intriguing mystery lady among the boisterous post-theatre crowd of well-dressed locals, longtime expats, international tourists, and amiably gruff French barmen. Cocktails €10.

Murano Urban Resort

13 BOULEVARD DU TEMPLE, 3RD.
TEL 01 42 71 20 00. FAX 01 42 71 21 01.
Mº FILLES DU CALVAIRE
WWW.MURANORESORT.COM

One of the hottest bars in the über-hip NoMa (North Marais) district is generously endowed with a 50-foot black slate bar – the longest in Paris. Not that a lady would be impressed by size alone: the bar serves over 160 varieties of vodka from all over the world as well as 30 cocktails created by the resident bar mistress, Sandrine. The stylish after-work crowd comes for the nightly live DJ sets and the popular Sunday afternoon jazz brunches. Settle yourself into the colorful retro swivel chairs or strike a pose on the 23-foot white leather Chesterfield sofa, prime location for spying your very own international man of mystery. Cocktails €16, Dinner €35-€60. *For hotel information see* **Your Boudoir or Mine?**

Speed Dating à la Française

If you're curious about the singles scene in Paris and feel confident enough flirting en français, why not sign up for a Turbo Dating party? They take place twice a week in a lounge bar near the Champs-Elysées, with age-specific evenings (20-35, 30-45, etc.). Entry is less expensive for the ladies, and includes drinks. The 10-minute "meetings" take place early in the evening, followed by dancing. Pre-register online at www.turbo-dating.com.

A Note for Solo Ladies

Upscale hotels usually have excellent bars frequented by both guests and locals. But don't take it personally if you're accidentally mistaken for a "working girl" if you're not a guest. Palace hotels in particular are notorious pickup grounds for these well-dressed ladies of the night and their lonely business traveling clientele.

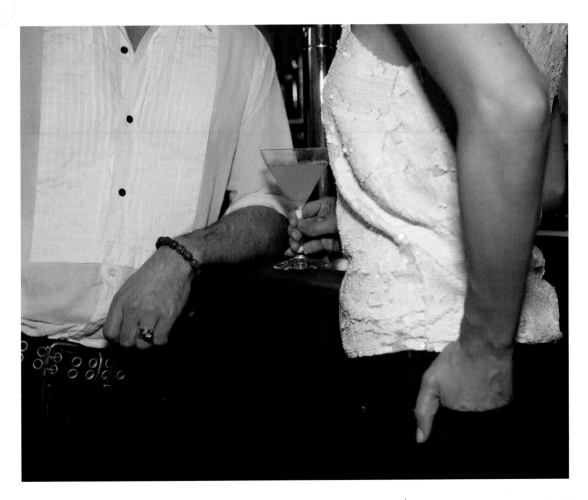

FLÛTE L'ETOILE

19 RUE DE L'ETOILE, 17TH.
Mº CHARLES DE GAULLE – ETOILE
TEL 01 45 72 10 14
WWW.FLUTEBAR.COM

A note for our gallant *Messieurs*: nothing makes us ladies swoon faster than Champagne. And this tiny new bar hidden on a side street near the Arc de Triomphe has over 120 different brands of bubbly, including over a dozen served by the glass. Take a seat in the dark and cozy mezzanine, with a view of the beautiful Champagne-bubble inspired chandelier. The Franco-American owners opened the original Flûte in Manhattan ten years ago, and have imported their exotic bar snacks and cocktails with names like "Marquis de Sade" and "Antoinette". And at these prices, anyone can afford to indulge. Bottles from €50, glasses from €9. Cocktails €12.

LA MEZZANINE AT ALCAZAR

62 RUE MAZARINE, 6TH.
Mº ODÉON
TEL : 01 53 10 19 99
WWW.ALCAZAR.FR

Forget *gauche*. The Left Bank can be just as fashionable as the other side of the Seine if you know where to look. The small, nondescript doorway on the narrow street between St-Germain-des-Prés and St-Michel doesn't look promising. But once inside you'll find a surprisingly spacious, contemporary restaurant with a distinct London vibe. Follow the stairs up to the Mezzanine lounge bar, where you and the ladies can comfortably spread out and enjoy your mojitos while surveying the arrival of the power-suited after-work crowd. Live DJs raise the volume on the sociable atmosphere Wednesday through Saturday. Divide and conquer, *Mesdames*. Cocktails €12, Appetizers €8-€20.

BOUND

49 AVENUE GEORGE V, 8TH.
M° GEORGE V
TEL 01 53 67 84 60
WWW.BOUND.FR

Just a precious stone's throw from the Louis Vuitton flagship store on the Champs-Elysées, this glam rock lounge bar is the perfect place to unwind with the ladies after an afternoon of window shopping in the Golden Triangle. The immense space has a New York atmosphere, with contemporary art scenes on plasma screens and Venetian chandeliers suspended from the high ceilings. Pile comfortably into one of the huge metallic leather booths or rub shoulders with Parisian businessmen at the hot pink bar. The house sushi bar will help you keep an eye on that girlish figure, if not your budget. Cocktails €10-€16 Dinner €40-€60.

LE BAR DU PLAZA ATHÉNÉE

25 AVENUE MONTAIGNE, 8TH.
M° ALMA MARCEAU
TEL 01 53 67 66 65
WWW.PLAZA-ATHENEE-PARIS.COM

Go ahead. Wear those oversized Versace shades and fabulously tall stilettos. You can't possibly overdress at the Plaza Athénée, preferred stomping grounds of the bling-laden international jetset and Carrie's *pied-à-terre* for the *Sex and the City* series finale. Catwalk through the ritzy gallery to the hotel bar, where a surprising mix of old world architecture and avant-garde design creates a becoming setting for you and the ladies. Have a round of Jelly Shots at the glowing "iceberg" bar, then settle into one of the giant picture frame seats with a Fashion Ice Cosmopolitan…a veritable *tableau vivant*. Cocktails €17-€25. Appetizers €26.

Ladurée is for Ladies

This is a salon du thé, not a bar, but as far as naughty indulgences go, Ladurée is every lady's dream. From the elegantly sumptuous décor to the exquisite pastries and rich hot chocolate, it's almost impossible to resist coming here more than once a day… so why even try? It takes time to test every single divine flavor of macaron. The Champs-Elysées location (75 avenue des Champs-Elysées, 8th, tel 01 40 75 08 75) is open 7:30 a.m. until midnight.

With your Beau

These bars are all conveniently conducive for a secluded *tête-à-tête* with your lover, but if you're still not sure whether *Monsieur* measures up, keep your options open by joining him for "just an aperitif" at one of the restaurant bars listed here. If you decide to find out where that naughty twinkle in his eye might lead, you can allow him the pleasure of convincing you to stay for dinner.

The proper way to order Champagne

"Un coup, s'il vous plait." Never *un verre!*

WINI JUNE
16 RUE DUPETIT-THOUARS, 3RD.
M° TEMPLE OR RÉPUBLIQUE
TEL 01 44 61 76 41

An island of elegance in the newly trendy Temple district of the Marais, this inviting and feminine lounge bar is an intimate gathering place for the fashionable few. The statuesque blonde Wini has given her tiny establishment the feel of a private living room, decorated with Venetian mirrors, pretty flea market finds, mismatched antique tables and cozy armchairs. Savor the candlelit ambience with your lover over chiseled crystal glasses of Champagne. Cocktails €10.

BUBAR
3, RUE DES TOURNELLES, 4TH.
M° BASTILLE
TEL 01 40 29 97 72

There's no sign outside this inconspicuous wine bar on the edge of the Marais, which is how the regulars like it. But once inside you'll find a welcoming and unpretentious atmosphere of 30-something locals. Soft jazz and flattering lighting encourage close conversation, and the charming owner is always ready to help newcomers choose from the extensive list of international wines. Far from being a meat-market, solo ladies will feel comfortable here, making it a perfect place to arrange your first *rendez-vous* in case your French date is fashionably late or —— *horreur!* —— unfashionably pulls a no-show. Wine €3-€7/glass.

LE BAR

25 RUE DE CONDÉ, 6TH.
M° ODÉON
TEL 01 43 29 06 61

You walk, arm-in-arm, away from the boisterous
bars and cinemas of the Place de l'Odéon, past the
imposing theatre where the scandalous *Marriage of
Figaro* was first performed, towards the Jardins du
Luxembourg. Your Parisian lover insists *"Il n'y a pas de
bar ici…"* But you know better. A discreet entrance, a
friendly welcome at the bar, a large menu of cocktails
and Champagne. Couples take advantage of the warren
of darkened rooms, where exotic, spot-lit African and
Asian statues provide the only illumination necessary
for finding each other's lips. Cocktails €9.

L'HOTEL

13 RUE DES BEAUX-ARTS, 6TH.
M° ST-GERMAIN-DES-PRÉS
TEL 01 44 41 99 00
WWW.L-HOTEL.COM

After a day of browsing the art galleries of St-Germain-
des-Prés, duck into this dark and sumptuous hotel bar
to steal kisses over snifters of Cognac. Designer Jacques
Garcia has richly decorated the interior with leopard
print carpeting, purple velvet sofas, and silk taffeta wall
coverings. If this luxurious excess whets your appetite
for more, move into the adjacent restaurant for a fine
meal of seasonal French classics, beautifully presented
with contemporary flair. Secure a romantic patio table
with a call to the concierge in advance. Cocktails €10-
€14, Dinner €40-€70. *For hotel information see **Your
Boudoir or Mine?***

LA CLOSERIE DES LILAS

171 BOULEVARD MONTPARNASSE, 6TH.
Mᵒ VAVIN OR RER PORT-ROYAL
TEL 01 40 51 34 50
WWW.CLOSERIEDESLILAS.NET

Montparnasse might not be the artistic and literary haven it was in the 1920s, but the thick hedge separating this legendary establishment from the busy boulevards seems to have preserved the dignified weight of its history. Take a seat in the cozy piano bar, a masculine refuge of polished mahogany, glowing red lamps, and leather-upholstered chairs once frequented by Beckett, Fitzgerald, Hemingway, Rimbaud, Sartre, and Man Ray. Is that hunger in his eyes? Try and behave during a formal French feast in La Closerie's garden restaurant, or tantalize more than his taste buds with an aphrodisiacal platter of oysters in the laid-back brasserie. Glass of Cognac €13, Dinner €30-€50.

LE LUP

2 RUE DU SABOT, 6TH.
Mᵒ ST-GERMAIN-DES-PRÉS
TEL 01 45 48 86 47
WWW.LELUP.COM

It's almost 2 a.m. and you're suddenly famished. Time flies when you're having fun, *non*? When late-night cravings strike, be sure to have this address tucked into your purse. Hidden on a tiny street in St-Germain-des-Prés, this red quilted refuge for Parisian *noctambules* serves an eclectic menu of fusion cuisine from 9pm until 5am, Wednesday through Saturday. Diners are seated in the candlelit mezzanine overlooking the cocktail lounge, where live jazz musicians perform nightly. Dinner €40-€70.

PERSHING HALL

49, RUE PIERRE CHARRON, 8TH.
Mº FRANKLIN D. ROOSEVELT
TEL 01 58 36 58 36
WWW.PERSHINGHALL.COM

First impressions count. Beyond the graceful 19th-century façade, a large doorway leads you through a tunnel of colored lights and beaded glass curtains to a striking, contemporary interior. DJs play chilled lounge tunes upstairs in the Pershing Lounge, where glamorous clientele sip cocktails under the glow of Murano glass chandeliers. For dinner, reserve a private table for you and *Chéri* in one of the wrought-iron balconies. The Asian fusion cuisine is tasty enough, but it's the view over the courtyard's dramatic vertical garden that will leave a lasting impression. Cocktails €15-20. Dinner €50-100.

BAR ECLAIREUR
10, RUE BOISSY D'ANGLAS, 8TH.
Mº CONCORDE
TEL 01 53 43 03 70
WWW.LECLAIREUR.COM

JAIPUR BAR
AT HOTEL VERNET
25 RUE VERNET, 8TH.
Mº CHARLES DE GAULLE- ETOILE
TEL 01 44 31 98 00
WWW.HOTELVERNET.COM

Hiding in the passage between the cutting-edge Eclaireur boutique and the famous Buddha Bar, this remarkable restaurant-bar evokes the witty retro world of the late Italian surrealist Piero Fornasetti. At first glance, the whimsical yet refined setting seems innocent enough for a respectable glass of wine. But if your date has a keen eye he'll soon spot Piero's erotic drawings hanging in one corner, or the cheeky 1950s prints etched onto the barstools. Suggestive, yes, but not silly. Exotic cocktails have names like Monkey Cane and Old Teenager, and the gourmet menu captures the refreshing flavors of southern Italy. Cocktails €13 Dinner €30-€50.

He said discretion was an absolute must, and slipped the address of this hotel into her pocket. "*Ce soir, dans le bar*," he whispered. She strolled along the Champs-Elysées later that evening, turned down a quiet side street, and almost missed the elegant marble entrance. Stairs on the left, lit by tiny candles, led her down into the Jaipur, a softly-lit lounge bar with an exotic Indian décor of ruby red walls, dark wood paneling, and Oriental rugs. They shared a plate of foie gras, and later, feeling more daring in their secluded corner, ordered an Absinthe nightcap. Cocktails €8-€15. Dinner €20-€45.

SIR WINSTON
5 RUE DE PRESBOURG, 16TH.
M° CHARLES DE GAULLE- ETOILE
TEL 01 40 67 17 37

Everyone can't help but look good in this dark and sultry whisky bar, decorated in British colonial style with leather chesterfields and Buddha statues. Trendy lounge music and incense permeate the bar and restaurant where international businessmen of the Champs-Elysées district mingle with fashion-conscious ladies sporting the latest "It" bag. Forget about them. Lead your lover downstairs to one of the leopard-print booths where you'll have ample privacy for advanced games of footsie, or —— depending on the hour and how many cocktails you've downed —— a very illicit tryst. Whisky €8-€10.

LE FIRST BOUDOIR
WESTIN HOTEL, 234 RUE DE RIVOLI, 1ST.
M° TUILERIES
TEL 01 44 77 10 40
WWW.LEFIRSTRESTAURANT.COM

A runway of tiny candles line the dark, wood-paneled passage between the upscale Westin and its contemporary "boudoir restaurant" overlooking the Tuileries Gardens. Reserve a table along the back wall, where you can sit side by side in the plush violet velour banquettes with a view of the candlelit room, decorated with deep mauve walls and shaded lamps. Neighboring conversations and the traffic outside are muffled by the thick carpeting and low ceilings. Order the chef's gourmet tasting menu, and you'll have seven leisurely courses to decide whether or not to continue your adventures *ensemble*. Contemporary and refined French brasserie cuisine, €35-75.

Intimate Dining à Deux

There's something to be said for the city's scruffy-yet-charming bistros where you're literally rubbing shoulders with the natives packed in next to you. But we're not going to say it here. When you only have eyes for each other, these low-lit restaurants will surely whet your appetite for seduction.

Dusk-to-Dawn Delivery

France is not a country of 24-hour supermarkets and drugstores, so what's a lady to do when she runs out of life's essentials between 7 p.m. and 6 a.m.? You could try room service, but they'll find it hard to compete with Nemo, the luxury "Night Provider." Foie gras, caviar, wine, Champagne (with the flutes for serving and ice cubes to keep it chilled), ice cream, flowers, even hot meals and Continental breakfast are delivered to your hotel or apartment within the hour. But best of all, Nemo also delivers Plaisirs Chics – condoms and sex toys – as well as "Sleep-Over" kits that include an extra pair of stockings, g-string, make-up remover and tooth brush for her, or boxers, socks, and a razor for him. Convenience has its price, specifically a €30 minimum for deliveries, payment accepted by credit card. Order online at www.nemo-paris.com or call 01 47 23 43 37.

Carpe Diem Café

21 RUE DES HALLES, 1ST.
Mº CHÂTELET OR PONT NEUF
TEL 01 42 21 02 01
WWW.CARPEDIEMCAFE.FR

Seize the night at this cozy café near Les Halles, where tasty French dishes are served under an inky blue ceiling dotted with fiber optic stars. Large windows, wooden floors and a neo-retro bar where stylish locals sit reading the paper create a friendly, informal atmosphere. You and your date, however, will be escorted to a table more conducive to creating chemistry, either in the sunken dining room or the more secluded mezzanine level surrounded by red velour curtains. Dine on roasted rib steak with Guérande salt, sesame chicken salad, or the house specialty of camembert grilled in caramelized cider. Dinner €30-45.

Le 404

69, RUE DES GRAVILLIERS, 3RD.
Mº ARTS-ET-MÉTIERS
TEL 01 42 74 57 81

"We'll always have Paris." But you don't have to go all the way to Casablanca to reenact Bogart and Bergman's cinematic chemistry. Raï music, incense, and lively conversation give this trendy restaurant on the edge of the Marais the exotic atmosphere of a North African souk. The clientele sit at low tables, surrounded by flickering candles and intricately carved woodwork, dining on authentic Berber cuisine of lamb tagine with prunes, couscous, spicy harissa, vegetable stews and grilled meats served in earthen clay pots. Reserve your dinner after 10 p.m., when the festive mood notches down to a simmer. Dinner €40-60.

Note: After dinner, head next door to the hip bar Andy Wahloo ("I have nothing" in Arabic) for a nightcap.

LAPÉROUSE

51 QUAI DES GRANDS AUGUSTINS, 6TH.
Mº ST-MICHEL
TEL 01 43 26 68 04
WWW.RESTAURANTLAPEROUSE.COM

The *maitre'd* escorted her through the historic 18th-century townhouse, up winding staircases and a maze of rooms decorated with antique furnishings, oil paintings, and intricately-carved woodwork. Her lover was waiting in a private salon overlooking the Seine, elegantly set for two. They dined on asparagus carpaccio in truffle oil, lobster salad, Bresse chicken, and praline soufflé with hot caramel and rum sauce. She traced a finger along the hearts and initials etched into the ancient mirrors. "How romantic," she sighed as the *digestifs* arrived. "The famous courtesans of the Second Empire used to meet their lovers here," he murmured, joining her on the velvet sofa. "They were simply testing the authenticity of their diamonds." "Well, a lady needs to know where she stands," she replied with a naughty wink. Dinner €95-120.

LES OMBRES

MUSÉE DU QUAI BRANLY, 27 QUAI BRANLY, 7TH.
RER PONT ALMA
TEL 01 47 53 68 00
WWW.LESOMBRES-RESTAURANT.COM

Champagne, diamonds, the Eiffel Tower…we ladies adore anything that sparkles. Jean Nouvel's striking steel and glass panoramic restaurant atop the Quai Branly Museum has prime views of the dazzling Iron Lady, no matter where you're sitting. If you can tear your eyes away from the breathtaking surroundings, peruse the seasonal menu of light and modern French gastronomic dishes such as sardines stuffed with baby spinach, Basque style piquillo peppers, cinnamon roasted duck, artichoke *millefeuille*, and green tea macaroons. Reserve well in advance for the more intimate outdoor tables (weather permitting). Contemporary, semi-formal setting. Dinner €65-95.

See **Get in the Mood** *for museum information.*

BLACK CALAVADOS

40 AVENUE PIERRE 1RE DE SERBIE, 8TH.
M° ALMA MARCEAU
TEL 01 47 20 77 77
WWW.BC-PARIS.FR

"There's something about this that's so black, it's like, how much more black could this be?"
—SPINAL TAP

You know you look drop dead gorgeous in black, so get thee to the Black Calavados, aka *Le BC*, where hard rock meets high fashion in the posh Golden Triangle district. Glossy black walls accentuated by crisp white tablecloths, smoked mirrors and retro lighting create a sexy setting where both cutting-edge fashionistas and tattooed musicians in tee shirts feel relaxed. With a nod to the owners' American roots (*le ravissant* rocker Chris Cornell among them), the daring menu has everything from gourmet munchies such as lobster hot dogs and truffle pizza to inventive haute cuisine such as caramelized black cod and foie gras tournedos with black beans. With service until 3 a.m., it's the perfect place to fuel between nocturnal frolickings. Dinner €40-€70.

Black List? The guarded black doorway outside leads down to the BC's private bar-club. You could always try to get past the stern doorman after dinner, but without an invitation or the right "look," don't get your hopes up.

GINGER

11 RUE DE LA TRÉMOILLE, 8TH.
Mᵒ ALMA MARCEAU
TEL 01 47 23 37 32

I have the right to love many people at once and to change my prince often.

—ANAÏS NIN

According to French legend, the famous royal mistress Madame du Barry served ginger as an aphrodisiac to all of her lovers at Versailles, including King Louis XV. Modern seductresses will find the stimulating spice used liberally in the cuisine of this fashionable Thai-Vietnamese restaurant. The fresh and contemporary take on traditional Asian dishes make it popular with Parisian models and actresses looking to maintain their silhouettes, but the flattering candlelight makes everyone look good. Start with a strong house cocktail at the bar, then move to one of the quiet tables in the back. If his desire requires further encouragement, the Crazy Horse is just around the corner. Dinner €40-60.

Note: French palates being as delicate as they are, the flavors may be more subtle than what you're accustomed to; be sure to let the charming servers know if you prefer your dish très epicée.

CRISTAL ROOM BACCARAT

11 PLACE DES ETATS-UNIS, 16TH.
M° IÉNA
TEL 01 40 22 11 10
WWW.BACCARAT.FR

One of the greatest art patrons of the 20th century, Viscountess Marie-Laure de Noailles descended from an illustrious family of bankers and aristocrats, including the infamous Marquis de Sade. The Second Empire mansion where she threw her legendary parties from 1920-1970 is now home to the Maison Baccarat, incorporating an ultra-modern showroom, gallery, and restaurant designed by Philippe Starck. The setting is chic and enchanting, with raw brick walls, ancient parquet floors, and luxurious crystal chandeliers endlessly reflected in gilt-framed mirrors. The menu of nouveau-Gallic cuisine changes monthly. Reserve a private table (not one of the uncomfortable banquettes) well in advance. Dinner €50-€120.

Especially Naughty Dining

AUTREMENT ...CHEZ SOI

97, RUE DE CLÉRY, 2ND.
M° BONNE NOUVELLES
TEL 01 47 03 09 14
WWW.AUTREMENT-CHEZ-SOI.COM

Attention! This is not a swingers club; playmates must stick together and solo wanderings once inside are forbidden.

The French might not shy away from public displays of affection, but it would be in very poor taste to attempt anything more than a lingering kiss in most Parisian restaurants. But couples are welcomed to make themselves "at home… in a different way" at *Autrement… Chez Soi*, a restaurant and lounge bar catering to the exhibitionist — and by extension voyeuristic — inclinations of its clientele. The narrow, 17th-century townhouse has five small rooms, one on each floor, where up to twenty couples (or trios) can come day or night for anything from an intimate meal in the restaurant, Champagne and caviar in the lounge, erotic pole dancing, or a romp in the "bedroom." The candlelit rooms are decorated with a mix of tasteful period and contemporary furnishings, covered in satin, velour, and leopard prints. Mirrors reflect steamy embraces and illicit caresses from all angles; no one requires you to show off your own moves, but watching is certainly encouraged. Check out the website for regularly scheduled theme parties (masked ball, lingerie trunk shows, striptease lessons…).

Naughty Notes: No entry fee, but the dress code must be respected (suits for men and sexy heels and skirts or dresses for ladies – changing rooms available). Reservations required. Dinner €75-100. Restaurant open for lunch (noon-4 p.m.) and dinner (from 9 p.m.); lounge open from 9 p.m., dance floor open from 11 p.m.. Ladies-only parties with male entertainment available for groups from €100/person.

A Note on PDA

"If we did this where I come from, it would be called PDA," she whispered into her French lover's ear. "Public Display of Affection." He looked shocked, and got very serious for a moment. "It sounds like a disease." Then he laughed. "I'm not kidding," she replied, sighing as he ran his hands down her back and kissed her neck. "They would scold us. 'Get a room!' they would say...." The lovers found themselves a bench under the trees of a quiet square, and kissed as the sky darkened with the setting sun, oblivious to the passers-by, who seemed likewise unaware. Except for one elderly gentleman, who began serenading the lovers with a joyous Georges Brassens song, *Les Amoureux des Bancs Publics* (Lovers on the Public Benches).

DANCING DIVA

Dance your last tango in Paris...

Flash & Fun

The glory days of the classic Parisian *discothèques* peaked in the 1990s, but the hype lives on for girls who just wanna have fun. So dress to the nines and boogie down until dawn with the all-ages crowd in a festive atmosphere. Expect icy doormen, expensive entrance fees, and generic dance music hits for an international crowd of all ages. Wear your oversized sunglasses to shield your eyes from the bling, and never, ever arrive before midnight unless you want to be the first one on the dance floor.

Le Cab

2 PLACE DU PALAIS ROYAL, 1ST.
M° PALAIS ROYAL
TEL 01 58 62 56 25
WWW.CABARET.FR

Sleek and futuristic, with cozy padded nooks and DJ music ranging from house and hip hop to 80s and disco. Reserve a table at the restaurant to bypass the doormen. Open Thursday-Saturday nights.

Le Showcase

UNDER THE PONT ALEXANDRE III, 8TH.
M° CHAMPS ELYSÉES-CLEMENCEAU
TEL 01 45 61 25 43
WWW.SHOWCASE.FR

There's plenty of space to dance and intermingle in this spacious club built under the stone arches of the historic Tsar Alexandre III bridge. Live bands and international DJs attract a predominantly young and trendy Parisian crowd every Friday and Saturday from 10 p.m. until dawn.

Le Queen

102 AVENUE DES CHAMPS-ELYSÉES, 8TH.
M° GEORGE V
TEL 01 53 89 08 90
WWW.QUEEN.FR

No longer just for the boys, on Wednesday nights this legendary Champs-Elysées club has free entry, open bar and makeovers for the ladies (and special bracelets for singles to help facilitate flirting). Come on Monday night for the best disco soirée in town.

L'Etoile

12 RUE DE PRESBOURG, 16TH.
M° CHARLES DE GAULLE – ETOILE
TEL 01 45 00 78 70
WWW.LETOILEPARIS.COM

This exclusive club in the shadow of the Arc de Triomphe is frequented by Parisian glitterati and young things sporting daddy's Platinum card. Come on Tuesdays for the Girl's Privilege night, with open cocktail bar and special gifts for the ladies.

Happy Hour Soirées

If you don't want to wait until midnight to go dancing, join the young Parisian suit-and-tie brigade for one of the Urban Nights' "After Work" parties in the city's swankiest nightclubs, every Thursday from 7 p.m. until 1 a.m., with open bar and buffet until 9 p.m. Locations announced each week at www.urban-nights.com. Entry €15 if you bring a printout of the web flyer.

Selective & Seductive

If you're not one to mingle with the masses and have a gift for charming your way past the velvet rope, then you might gain entrance to the sexy and intimate confines of these exclusive Parisian venues. The dance floors are small – quality over quantity *oblige* – but entry is free. If you're not on the "list," come before midnight and be prepared to wait patiently for the doorman's nod of approval.

CHEZ CASTEL

15, RUE PRINCESSE, 6TH.
Mº MABILLON
TEL 01 40 51 52 80

Playground of the posh Parisian jetset, this renowned private club on the Left Bank has been turning people away for over 40 years. Have your concierge reserve a table, and don't come without a date unless you're ready to fend off indecent proposals by aging playboys. Open Thursday-Saturday.

NEO CLUB

23 RUE DU PONTHIEU, 8TH.
Mº FRANKLIN D. ROOSEVELT
TEL 01 42 25 57 14
WWW.NEOCLUB.COM

Models, rockers and film stars with a rebellious streak appreciate the edgy New York/Los Angeles vibe of this contemporary club off the Champs-Elysées. Hard liquor and hardcore music keep the dance floor crowd fueled until the wee hours Thursday through Saturday.

Le Baron
6 AVENUE MARCEAU, 8TH.
Mᵒ ALMA-MARCEAU
TEL 01 47 20 04 01

This former gentlemen's club still has its boudoir décor of red velour and risqué vintage photographs. Despite an A-list clientele, the atmosphere is surprisingly unpretentious. Whether you're at the bar, on the dance floor or in the bathrooms, be prepared to suck it in as you plunge through the heaving crowd of trendy young party animals.

You will do foolish things, but do them with enthusiasm.
——COLETTE

Live & Laid Back

Want to shake your booty but avoid the hassle of dress codes and snobby bartenders? These typically Parisian live music venues are perfect for finding dance partners in a more casual and inclusive setting for all ages.

LA DAME DE CANTON

QUAI FRANÇOIS MAURIAC, 13TH.
M° QUAI DE LA GARE OR BIBLIOTHÈQUE
TEL 01 44 06 96 45
WWW.DAMEDECANTON.COM

Permanently moored on the banks of the Seine, this whimsical barge is actually an old Chinese sailing junk converted into a pirate ship. Monsieur Depp may not be clinging to the mast, but you can conveniently cling to the nearest available hottie as the boat rocks to the rhythms of World Music, rock, reggae and jazz. Live concerts every weekend followed by a DJ for dancing until dawn.

L'ELYSÉE DE MONTMARTRE

72, BOULEVARD DE ROCHECHOUART, 18TH.
M° ANVERS
TEL 01 44 92 45 47
WWW.ELYSEEMONTMARTRE.COM

Open since 1807, the Elysée Montmartre has an illustrious place in Parisian history as the birthplace of the French Cancan. Dancing is still an important aspect of this concert hall, with top international DJs every weekend, but the real draw is "Le Bal de l'Elysée," a very French dance party featuring a live ten-piece band who perform classic disco, funk, rock, and pop hits from the '60s to the '90s. The atmosphere is fun and friendly, with Parisians of all ages dancing together. Every other Saturday from 11:30 p.m., entry €17.

Retro & Latin Moves

Whether you're dying to shake your booty with the sultans of swing or dream about dancing your last tango in Paris, these exceptional and historical venues can satisfy all of your exotic and retro dance cravings.

Dancing Resources

For the most up-to-date news on Tango and Salsa events and classes in Paris, check out www.tango-argentin.net and www.salsafrance.com. If you understand French, try calling the **Allo-Danse** hotline for all dancing events in Paris, 08 92 70 50 25 (€.034/minute).

OPEN-AIR DANCING
SQUARE TINO ROSSI, QUAI ST BERNARD, 5TH.
Mº JUSSIEU

There's something magical about dancing on the banks of the Seine, the swirling couples lit up by sightseeing boats and Notre Dame Cathedral in the background. Four small amphitheatres welcome tango, salsa, swing and even Brittany folk dancers of all ages and abilities. Every evening May through September, from sunset through midnight. Free entry.

WAGG

62 RUE MAZARINE, 6TH.
Mº ODÉON
TEL 01 53 10 19 99
WWW.WAGG.FR
WWW.TUMBAOPROD.COM

The vaulted stone cellars of the former Whisky à Go Go where singer Jim Morrison spent his last hours in 1971 now host a modern Parisian dance club playing house, dtco, and classic '80s dance music for a predominantly 20- and 30-something crowd. But on Sunday it becomes a Cuban salsa club, with classes from 3-5 p.m. followed by dancing until 2am. There's little space for wallflowers to sit, so come with your dancing shoes. Class and entry, €12.

BARRIO LATINO

46 RUE DU FAUBOURG ST-ANTOINE, 12TH.
Mº BASTILLE
TEL 01 55 78 84 75
WWW.BUDDHABAR.COM

A magnificent setting of wood and wrought iron, this refurbished factory designed by Gustave Eiffel has four levels connected by a grand staircase, decorated in typical Havana style with leather club chairs, colorful lanterns, and ochre walls. Smartly-dressed locals show off their moves on the tiny dance floor to bossa-nova, mambo and salsa beats. Monday-Saturday until 11 a.m. – 2 a.m., Sundays 3-7:30 p.m. Entry €5.

LE BALAJO

9 RUE DE LAPPE, 11TH.
Mº BASTILLE
TEL 01 47 00 07 87

Open since 1936, this authentic dance hall with the historic Parisian street scene decor was where French crooners like Edith Piaf used to sing. Couples and singles decked out in vintage duds come on Wednesday nights for the '40s and '50s swing-rock evenings. Thursdays are for salsa dancing and the last Sunday of the month for tango.
Call to confirm times; entry €12.

BISTRO LATIN

20 RUE DU TEMPLE, 3RD.
Mº HÔTEL DE VILLE
TEL 01 42 77 21 11
WWW.BISTROTLATIN.COM

On the edge of the Marais, above Le Latina movie theatre, serious tango and salsa aficionados come together on the parquet dance floor to live out their Latin Lover fantasies six nights a week: Tango Wednesday-Saturday, salsa dancing Sunday, and Sevillana dancing Monday. From 8:30 p.m. until 1 a.m.; come early for lessons. Entry €6 (€9 Saturday for the live music).

Le Quart d'Heure Américain

Remember the school dance when the lights would go down and the DJ would play those sappy old love songs? In France they call this *Le Quart d'Heure Américain*, literally, "The American Quarter-hour," and the women are expected to choose their dance partner. "Slows" are horribly out of fashion these days, but that doesn't mean you can't take the initiative and invite the nearest eligible hottie onto the dance floor.

SEXY SHOWS

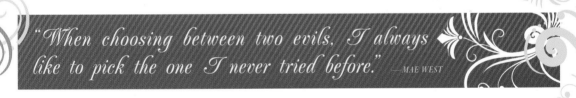

"When choosing between two evils, I always like to pick the one I never tried before." —MAE WEST

Cabarets & Striptease

Paris has a rich and varied calendar of performing arts includes sensual ballets, passionate operas, and riveting theatre. But ever since Toulouse-Lautrec immortalized the scandalous high-kicks of the French Cancan, no one can resist the siren song of the city's world famous cabarets. From sassy to shocking, engaging to erotic, there's certainly one that fits your mood...

LE CRAZY HORSE

12 AVENUE GEORGE V, 8TH.
Mº ALMA-MARCEAU OR GEORGE V
TEL 01 47 23 32 32
SHOWS SUN-FRI 8:30 P.M. AND 11 P.M.;
SAT 7:30 P.M., 9:45 P.M., AND 11:50 P.M.
WWW.LECRAZYHORSEPARIS.COM

Undeniably the sexiest cabaret in Paris, Crazy Horse is small and intimate, with a female-only dance troupe of heavenly identical bodies. Each scene, whether performed by a dozen dancers or a solo performer, is expertly choreographed to bring out the most enticing aspects of the feminine physique. The effect is mesmerizing and undeniably erotic. "The cabaret celebrates and glorifies women," explains Andrée Deissenberg, the passionate young Franco-American woman appointed General Director in 2005. "It doesn't look or feel raunchy. The women here feel beautiful and free…empowered. Proud to be a woman!" It's no surprise, then, that over half of the clientele are also women, perhaps hoping to learn a trick or two about how to make the most of their feminine wiles. Keep an eye out for special performances by famous guests, like burlesque strip-teaser Dita von Teese or the sexy French actress-singer Arielle Dombasle. Ambience oblige, there's no dinner service, no children under 18, and no busloads of tourists. Tickets from €100.

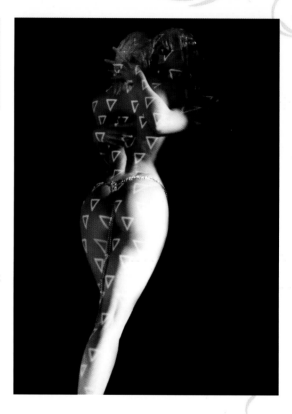

Tip: Even with advanced reservations, get there early for the best seats.

LE MOULIN ROUGE

82 BOULEVARD DE CLICHY, 18TH.
M° BLANCHE
TEL 01 53 09 82 82
SHOWS AT 9 P.M. AND 11 P.M. (DINNER SHOW BEGINS AT 7 P.M.).
WWW.MOULINROUGE.COM

The Moulin Rouge was an instant hit when it opened in 1889. Over a century later the scandalous French Cancan dance remains the highlight of the show, while other numbers have more of Broadway-with-Breasts feel to them, with an immense troupe of singing male and female dancers (*en français*, of course), supplemented by acrobats and magicians. The historical significance of the Moulin Rouge can't be denied, but the only thing shocking about this cabaret today is that such a family-friendly place (children as young as six admitted) still thrives in the seediest *quartier* of Paris. Tickets from €89. **Tip**: *Go to the late show, preferably off-season, to avoid the worst of the long lines.*

Moulin Rouge Souvenirs: Can't make it to the show? Pick up a few souvenirs from the Moulin Rouge boutique, just around the corner at 11 rue Lepic (open Tuesday-Saturday 10 a.m. – 7 p.m.).

BOBIN'O

20 RUE DE LA GAÎTÉ, 14TH.
M° EDGAR-QUINET
TEL 43 27 24 24
DOORS OPEN WEDNESDAY-SATURDAY AT 7:30 P.M. FOR THE DINNER-SHOW, AT 9 P.M. FOR CHAMPAGNE-SHOW. NIGHTCLUB OPEN FROM 11 P.M.
WWW.BOBINO.FR

Opened in summer 2007, today's Bobin'O is actually a contemporary reincarnation of a music hall that has existed in one form or another since 1812. Sexy like the Crazy Horse, entertaining like the Moulin Rouge, but with a generous dose of good humor and a dashing host who pulls it all together in style. The French know their cheese, so expect a bit of slapstick and drag queen antics alongside the talented male and female dancers. Ladies, hold onto your men or they may become part of the show. And unique to Bobin'O, after 11 p.m. the locals start arriving *en masse* as the cabaret is transformed into an immense nightclub with a live DJ until dawn. Tickets from €85.

Tip: Reserve the private Loges for 4 or 6 people for the best seats in the house, Champagne included.

And also…

- **Le Paradis Latin** (28 rue du Cardinal Lemoine, 5th, Tel 01 43 25 28 28, www.paradis-latin.com): The French prefer this attractive cabaret, not just because the cuisine is cooked in-house, but also because there's only one show per night, so they can linger afterwards to finish their Champagne without being rushed. Dinner show guests seated first, but latecomers get to sit under the dome of the more intimate mezzanine. Tickets from €82.
- **Le Lido** (116bis avenue des Champs-Elysées, 8th, Tel 01 40 76 56 10, www.lido.fr): This is the closest Paris comes to Vegas-style entertainment, not surprising since it's on one of the ritziest avenues in Paris. Elaborate scenes, flashy costumes, dancers and stuntmen…Will you be dazzled? Definitely. Seduced? It's all a matter of taste, of course. Tickets from €80.

Eye Candy for the Ladies ➔

We ladies can certainly appreciate the fine beauty of female cabaret dancers, but when it's time to turn up the heat, nothing compares to the finely-chiseled male physique. Especially when he knows what to do with it… expressly for *Madame's* appreciative gaze.

AU BONHEUR DES DAMES

RÉGINE'S CLUB
49 RUE PONTHIEU, 8TH.
Mº FRANKLIN D. ROOSEVELT
TEL 06 21 70 52 56
WWW.BONHEUR-DES-DAMES.COM
ORGANIZER :ANNE-SOPHIE BAILLET RELATIONSPUBLIQUES@REGINE-PARIS.COM

Leave behind any Puritan ideas of how to behave in the presence of a naked hunk of masculinity. The rules are different here in Paris, where not only are you allowed to look, but you're expected to touch. Yes, you too can cross swords with Zorro, dance with a sheik, or be rescued by a strapping young fireman. Every Thursday night from 9:30 p.m. until 10:45 p.m., Régine's welcomes 200 ladies for this free soirée which includes unlimited cocktails, dinner, a beauty bar, and an interactive show. Wear something slinky and sexy to get noticed by the doorman amongst the sea of 20-something gazelles, and sit towards the front if you want to be one of the lucky ladies chosen to participate. At 11:30 p.m. gentlemen are invited in for dancing to local DJs until dawn.

Naughty tip

A pretty little handheld fan will help you keep your cool and fits snugly into your clutch.

GIRLS IN THE CITY

PINK PARADISE
49-51 RUE DE PONTHIEU, 8TH.
M° FRANKLIN D. ROOSEVELT
TEL 01 58 36 19 20.
HTTP://WWW.PINKPARADISE.FR

Coincidentally located right next to Régine's Club, this American-style lap dancing club for gentlemen has monthly ladies' nights with pole-dancing lessons from the pro's, beauty make-overs, and a Chippendales show. The €35 entry fee includes three cocktails.

LATIN CORNER

27 RUE DE LA HUCHETTE, 5TH.
M° ST-MICHEL
TEL 01 43 54 16 04
WWW.LATINCORNERCAFE.COM

Located dead center of the young and vibrant Latin Quarter, this fun and informal lounge bar is the perfect place to come any night of the week for a bit of tongue-in-cheek entertainment with your friends. It might look like any other student bar from the outside if it weren't for the lacy bra hanging from the palm tree. Inside, the topless male servers — sometimes just in their undies — will playfully get the crowd wound up before the performance starts. Open nightly until 2 a.m., no cover. Happy hour 6 p.m. — 8 p.m.

A Note on Voyeurism

In the French language, gender is usually designated by a word's suffix, with "-eur" denoting the masculine, such as "danseur," and "-euse" denoting the feminine, such as "danseuse". So a woman who likes to watch would actually be a "voyeuse," not a voyeur. "But there are never female voyeurs," said one French gentleman, after explaining this to a young American traveler. "Oh really?" she replied, one eyebrow arched. "You really think women don't get pleasure out of just looking?" Ladies, maybe this is a secret we should keep to ourselves a bit longer...

X-Rated *Naughtiness*

CINÉMA LE BEVERLEY

14 RUE DE LA VILLE NEUVE, 2ND.
Mᵒ BONNE NOUVELLE
TEL 01 40 26 00 69
WWW.CINEBEVERLEY.COM

Remember the days before VCRs and cable TV, when the only way to see pornographic films was to don a trench coat and dark glasses and slink off to the local "adults-only" theatre? Today we can watch as much naughtiness as we want in the privacy of our own homes. But sometimes privacy just isn't the point. Le Beverley is the last cinema of its kind – the pornographic kind – in Paris, with a cult following of regulars who look as if they've been coming (oh my, no pun intended) since the 70s. Thursday and Saturday are "couples only" nights (from 11 p.m.), with occasional Friday themed nights. The evening begins innocently enough with an erotic poetry reading and then progresses into a stage show if any of the clientele feel inspired to perform. When the films get rolling, usually "classics" from the 70s or 80s, the clientele "in the mood" take advantage of the relative darkness to do things you'd normally get kicked out of a regular cinema for doing. You may be invited to join in the frolicking with couples in the next row, but no one minds if you just choose to watch. After all, *someone* has to be the audience, *non?*

Naughty Note

For those who really do want to risk getting kicked out, try the double-wide "love seats" at the MK 2 Bibliothèque Cineplex (168 avenue de France, 13th, www.mk2.com), or the dark and cozy upper balcony at the historic Max Linder Panorama (24 boulevard Poissonnière, 9th, www.maxlinder. com). Just don't think you're the first clever couple to attempt such risqué antics in a cinema.

NAUGHTY ADVENTURES

Invited one day to attend an orgy in Paris, the great French philosopher Voltaire accepted with pleasure. The next day, after reporting to his friends that he had enjoyed the experience, he was invited to attend another. He declined the invitation with the reply: "Ah no, my good friends, once a philosopher, twice a pervert."

Libertine Clubs

Now that you've taken your time to discover the many sensual and titillating delights of Paris – because a lady would never skip ahead to the naughtiest bits of the book first, *ahem* – you're finally ready to embark on some seriously sexy adventures of your own. What better place than Paris to let go of our sexual inhibitions and live out our wildest fantasies? Of course, just reading about libertine clubs may be as far as some of you ladies dare to tread, but go ahead and admit it: you're dying to know what it's really like inside, aren't you? Whether you're curious, hesitant, or downright gung ho to get a piece of the action, a thorough briefing will help properly prepare you for this uniquely naughty experience.

The Concept

Libertine clubs, also known as swinger or *échangiste* clubs, are places where consenting adults go to meet, mingle, *et plus si affinité…* and more if there's chemistry. *Et oui*, "more" means sex, ladies. Known commonly as "wife-swapping" in the 1970s, these clubs became popular with married suburbanites looking to inject a bit of excitement into their sex lives. Today anything goes, with sexually liberated singles, couples, and even triples coming together for mutual fun and pleasure.

What to Expect

At this point you might be imagining sordid orgies where you're expected to check your clothes at the door and surrender yourself to a crowd of sex-crazed strangers. Relax. The reality is a touch more sophisticated in Paris. Unlike many other libertine clubs around the world, here you're not expected to disrobe upon arrival. That would ruin the whole point of seduction, which – for the French – is part of the allure. Aside from a few erotic images decorating the walls, nothing is out of the ordinary at first glance. Like any other Parisian nightclub, there's a bar, a dance floor, sometimes a restaurant, where smartly-dressed men and sexy women engage in nothing more shocking than shameless flirtation. Of course, there's more than meets the eye.

Sitting at the bar of one of the city's most exclusive clubs is Janice, an elegant woman in her 40s from upstate New York who visits Paris – and its libertine clubs – whenever she has the opportunity. Her look is striking yet classy, with a sheer black blouse over a lacy bra, fitted black skirt, patent Chanel stilettos, and impeccably-painted ruby lips. "Libertine clubs are just like regular clubs except that you get to dress sexier and be more daring in a setting that gives you the freedom to do what you couldn't do in other clubs," she says with a naughty grin. "It's a safe environment where sexual activity is encouraged, but never required. What's fun is that you have the choice," she says as she discreetly surveys the crowd over a flute of Champagne. "Even if nothing happens, it's exciting just knowing that sex is a possibility." A very real possibility, which fosters an erotically-charged atmosphere of lingering glances, suggestive smiles and overt seduction as couples size up potential playmates.

Getting Friendly

And how to make it clear if you are interested in frolicking with fellow swingers? "At the bar or dance floor this is similar to any other club, by striking up conversation or dancing a bit closer," explains Janice. After a few cocktails and a bit of dirty dancing, most of the couples – sometimes alone, sometimes with another couple – disappear into the back rooms, or *salons*. Rooms might be small and dark for just one couple or large and mirrored for many couples to cavort side by side on large beds or mattresses. Sometimes there are rooms with locking doors and one-way mirrors or windows so that couples can engage in some very public displays of affection without the risk of anyone else asking to join in. Other rooms might even have a light bondage theme where you can tie up or lock your partner. There are often as many voyeurs as there are exhibitionists, watching others before they decide whether to participate or not.

Proper Etiquette

A soft caress on the arm (or the closest body part) is what usually constitutes a pass in the *salons*. You can caress back, or politely shake your head *non*. Some couples just go to have fun with each other, not to mix with others. In either case, it's important to respectfully communicate your boundaries. Don't be afraid to use body language if your French fails you. Be subtle when making a pass of your own, and never insist. "The secret to having a positive experience in any club is a relaxed attitude and a sense of humor," says Janice. "Stay open-minded, have fun, and don't get too offended by the inevitable invitations… or rebuffs."

Along with groping *sans* permission, drinks are forbidden in the back rooms, and loud conversations or laughing are frowned upon. If at any time you get uncomfortable, you can always excuse yourself and return to the bar or dance floor, where sexual escapades and nudity are *interdits*. On couples' only nights, men are typically not allowed to venture into the *salons* without their partners. If you're unsure about the correct protocol, don't be afraid to ask another couple. Your neophyte status is the perfect ice-breaker.

Who Goes?

You might be surprised. Not every Parisian has the inclination to check out the local libertine club, but there's also no shameful stigma assigned to those who do. "Even in upscale social circles some women may simply smile mysteriously if the subject comes up in conversation...neither confirming nor denying if they've ever visited," says Janice. "Certain clubs are very fashionable, so you may even see famous personalities." There's usually a mix of regulars, curious visitors, and those looking for something fun and out of the ordinary for a special night out. Those who frequent the more exclusive clubs are generally cultured and well-behaved, aged anywhere from 30 to 60 years old.

Getting In

Without exception, women must be in dresses or skirts, and men in suits. Sneakers and jeans won't do no matter how much you paid for them. Try and look like the type of person who might be carrying a Titanium AMEX card. Think classy, not trashy, lest anyone mistake you for a "working" girl. "To get in, dress pretty and stylish...anything goes if it's part of your fantasy," says Janice. "Good quality shoes are a must. Especially since they may be all the doorman can see under your trench coat." Heels are preferred to boots, and only sheer stockings, *s'il vous plaît*, if you must wear them at all. Even if you're young and good-looking, you may still get turned away with a cold "*Désolé, c'est privé.*" It could mean the club is already full or that a private group has indeed rented the club for the evening. Take it in good stride and try another club.

Naughty Note

By the way, don't confuse libertine clubs with fetish or S/M clubs. This is not the place to dress up in your dominatrix or slave costume.

Your First Time

The best approach is to go with an open mind and keep your expectations in check. Like any nightclub, the atmosphere will depend on the crowd on any given night. Go on "couples only" evenings if you want to avoid an overbalance of men to women, and get there early before it gets crowded so you can slowly acclimate to the setting. When in a couple, have your ground rules established in advance, not in the heat of the moment. If you make it past the doorman, you'll be asked to check your coats and wallets (for safety reasons). You'll be given a card with your name – or your sexy pseudonym – that you give to the bartender for your tab and pay on the way out. The back room action doesn't usually begin right away, so you can relax first at the bar or in the restaurant. Then just see where the mood takes you. Remember, you're never obliged to join in.

Health & Safety

Despite the sinfully decadent activities going on in the *salons*, the clientele of libertine clubs are generally more polite and well-behaved than in regular nightclubs. After all, a club's reputation is largely dependent on the comfort of its female clientele. Anyone displaying rude or pushy behavior will be escorted immediately to the door. And if one night of fun is all you're looking for, at least in a libertine club you never have to decide "his place or mine" or find yourself alone with a stranger. For health and hygiene, condoms and showers are freely available at libertine clubs, usually in the restrooms.

A Bit of Advice

A glass (or two) of Champagne may help you relax, but don't drink so much that your judgment will be affected. There's nothing ladylike about drunken debauchery, even in a libertine club.

What about Unaccompanied Women?

Fair or not, upscale clubs who don't want to be accused of bringing in prostitutes to "even out the male-female ratio" will sometimes turn away unaccompanied women. Try coming on a night when single men are admitted, and you may meet an eligible bachelor at the door who will agree to accompany you inside. **Warning**: you usually have to leave with the person you came in with, so make sure Romeo doesn't disappear into the back rooms when you're ready to go.

Three Clubs ⊕

There are many sex clubs in Paris, but only the best have been selected for you ladies. Particularly suited for newcomers, these exclusive and attractive establishments are located in upscale neighborhoods and frequented by a discerning clientele.

LES CHANDELLES
1, RUE THÉRÈSE, 1ST.
Mᵒ PYRAMIDES
TEL 01 42 60 43 31
WWW.LES-CHANDELLES.COM

On a quiet street between the Louvre and the Opéra is an unmarked entrance on a nondescript façade. Step inside the small foyer, under camera surveillance, and ring the buzzer on the imposing door. If Madame's heels are high enough and Monsieur's double Windsor knot tied convincingly, then perhaps Valéry, the demanding lady of the house, will grant you access into one of the most exclusive libertine clubs in Paris.

If you're one of the golden few to get inside, it's time to choose your own adventure. The stairs to the left lead past a sexy toy and lingerie boutique to the club's classy restaurant. To the right, another staircase leads to a red lounge room and its buffet of fruits and bon bons. Through the doorway to the right is the bar and dance floor. To the left are bathrooms and showers, and a curtained doorway which leads to the two low-lit and lushly-padded *salons*. Open passages on each side allow for discreet voyeuristic cruising. The décor, stylish and sophisticated, is changed regularly to keep up with the fickle tastes of its status-conscious clientele, predominantly pampered young beauties and moneyed gentlemen of a certain age. Don't be

surprised if you see familiar faces from film, fashion, music and even politics who come to "see and be seen," although – discretion *oblige* – what they're seen doing goes unsaid.

Hours & Rates
Monday to Saturday afternoons from 4-9 p.m. for "Après-midi Coquines." Entry €15 for couples (one drink each included), 39€ for singles (drink included).

Monday night from 10:30 p.m. for "Caprices de Femmes." Entry free for couples (drinks €15-€25), €100 for singles (drink included).
Tuesday to Saturday evenings from 10:30 p.m. for "Voluptés Nocturnes." Couples only, entry €76 (one drink each included).

Restaurant open Monday to Saturday from 9:30 p.m., average price à la carte €80, *menus* and club entry €110-€130 (drinks not included). Reservations necessary.

L'OVERSIDE

92 RUE CHERCHE MIDI, 6TH.
GALERIE LE SEVRIEN
Mº VANEAU
WWW.OVERSIDE.FR

While Les Chandelles represents the glamorous Right Bank, the Overside embraces the more youthful attitude of the Left Bank. At the entrance, located in a pedestrian passageway just off a fashionable shopping street, the *directrice* Danielle welcomes well-dressed couples who might be in their 20s or 60s, but are usually somewhere in the middle. The bar and dance floor have a sexy kitsch décor, with zebra-print bar stools and erotic statues of women in compromising positions. On the left through the black fringe curtains is the labyrinth of eight *salons*, including two which can be closed off for couples who don't want to be disturbed by anyone else. *La Fetish Zone* is equipped with a cage and bondage cross and the Greek-style *Salon Grec* has an elevated hexagonal bed used for the Soirée Massage, every first Friday of the month. A guard makes sure that single men don't enter the *salons* without a partner, although these rooms can become overwhelmingly crowded on the popular *Soirée Trio* nights. Still, the casual party atmosphere and more relaxed door policy make Overside a good choice for couples embarking on their inaugural libertine adventure.

Hours & Rates

Monday to Tuesday, Thursday to Saturday from 10:30 p.m. for "Soirée Couples". Entry €67 per couple (one drink each included).

Wednesday and Sunday "Soirée Trio," open from 8:30 p.m. for couples and from 10:30 p.m. for singles. Entry €54 for couples (one drink each included), €108 for single men (drink included). Open buffet from 9 p.m. Additional drinks €16.

LE NO COMMENT

36 RUE DE PONTHIEU, 8TH.
M° FRANKLIN D. ROOSEVELT
TEL 01 43 59 23 95
WWW.NOCOMMENTCLUB.COM

Just a few steps from the Avenue des Champs-Elysées on a street known for its exclusive night clubs, this chic libertine establishment attracts a refined, international crowd of all ages. The style is Art Deco but not kitsch, with wood-paneled walls, oil paintings, and wrought iron railings decorating several lounge areas where couples sit and socialize. It would feel more like a private living room than a nightclub if not for the large dance floor. This is one of the more spacious libertine clubs, spread out over three levels, but there are only five small *salons*, including one with an immense canopied bed strewn with zebra-print pillows. Two private rooms have a nautical theme with cheeky porthole windows so voyeurs can get an eyeful. Strictly reserved for couples only, try to arrive early on the busy weekend evenings.

Hours & Rates

Tuesday to Saturday from 11 p.m., couples only, €68 (one drink each included).

Restaurant open Thursday to Saturday from 9:30 p.m., €28 per person (drinks not included), reservations necessary.

Naughty Note: If you want to enjoy a bit of exhibitionist or voyeuristic fun without the pressure of sharing your man with anyone else – or steep entry fees – check out Autrement...Chez Soi (in the Intimate Dining à Deux section).

Fetish and Whips

Leather and latex and lace, *oh là la*! Welcome to the dark side, ladies. Perhaps you only turned to this page out of curiosity, believing fetish just isn't your thing. But you may have already, quite unknowingly, dabbled in fetish or sadomasochistic dalliances. Doth thou protest, *Madame*? Consider, if you will, the seemingly innocent satin blindfold next to your bed, the fuzzy handcuffs you purchased with a wicked giggle, and the sexy corset and stockings you wore for his birthday. If you've ever allowed yourself to be tied to the bedposts or left on your three-inch stiletto heels while making love, then you're not quite the "fetish virgin" you think you are.

Once considered strictly deviant and underground, today fetish and SM imagery have infiltrated popular culture, from Madonna's dominatrix influences and the neo-goth outfits in the Matrix to superheroes in skintight costumes and elaborate fantasy worlds of leather-clad warriors. And who doesn't love to vamp it up for Halloween? Safely disguised as our sexy alter egos, we become mysterious, intriguing, and audacious. We can be powerful with our vampire fangs, Catwoman claws, and Tomb Raider guns, or helpless damsels in distress at the mercy of dangerous pirates, devious devils, and whip-cracking jungle explorers.

Playing these Bad Girl/Bad Boy roles can be a huge turn on because, like in the movies or bodice-ripping novels, we know there isn't any real danger of getting hurt. Sexual tension builds during the drawn out power plays, inevitably leading to a pleasurable climax (pun intended) when the sparks start to fly. And this, dear ladies, is the same in the world of fetish and BDSM, albeit without the sad knowledge that you'll have to put your costumes away at the end until next Halloween.
Intrigued? Curious? Whether daring or undecided, you don't need to be a convert to the fetish lifestyle in order to enjoy an exploratory dabble in the Parisian scene, whose clubs and soirées are more accessible and female-friendly than you might expect. You may find a whole new world of sexy fun awaiting your discovery. Or, in the least, a memorable travel tale. But first, a few essential pointers on etiquette, dress code, and what to expect as a naughty neophyte.

Fetish vs BDSM? A Naughty Primer

BDSM is an umbrella acronym for activities that include Bondage/Discipline, Dominance/Submission, and Sadism/Masochism. There are subtle distinctions and overlapping between each practice, but in general BDSM is about psychological stimulation and physical sensations. It's an exchange of power based on trust with pleasure as the ultimate goal for both parties, even – despite appearances – when "pain" is involved. The important thing to keep in mind here is that it's nothing more than elaborate role play between consenting adults. Happily, for every man or woman who gets erotic pleasure out of tying up, whipping, and ordering someone else around, there's a soulmate out there who gets erotic pleasure out of being tied down, spanked, and obeying orders. Mmmmm...*la justice poétique.*

While BDSM concerns sexually arousing activities, fetishism is about sexually arousing objects such as high heels, seamed stockings, corsets, and clothing made from leather, rubber, latex, or PVC. Not all fetishists are into BDSM (and likewise, not all fetish soirées have dungeons for BDSM activities), however there's a lot of overlap between the two communities since many BDSM practitioners use fetish objects and wear fetish clothing. All of the SM clubs and soirées in Paris have a fetish dress code, mainly to deter gawking thrill-seekers who aren't into the "scene," so the umbrella term "Fetish" is used for all clubs and soirées, even when BDSM activities predominate.

Recommended References for your Naughty Library

Hungry for more information on the worlds of fetish and BDSM? These five books are a great place to start:

- *SM 101: A Realistic Introduction* by Jay Wiseman
- *Fetish Sex: An Erotic Guide for Couples* by Violet Blue
- *The Art of Sensual Female Dominance: A Guide for Women* by Claudia Varrin
- *The Mistress Manual: The Good Girl's Guide to Female Dominance* by Lorelei
- *Fetish and the Art of the Teese* by Dita von Teese

The Paris Scene

The fetish scene in Paris is primarily for those with a leather, latex or PVC fetish, and, as an extension, those who practice the BDSM lifestyle. This is the realm of fantasy, where you get to dress up, show off your "look," meet other likeminded fetishists, and realize your wildest dreams – all within the bounds of consensual participation and respect for the other guests. While libertine clubs are more about the unexpected and letting go for a night of fun, fetish parties are more like a stage for elaborate shows that are carefully rehearsed in advance, complete with role-playing, costumes, and an appreciative audience. Bondage and whipping scenes take on the feel of performance art, and the parade of fetish outfits may resemble the Parisian catwalk creations. But no matter how humble or flashy the event, these soirées are simply a way of bringing the underground into the open, where the thrill of being someone completely different in a very public setting adds to the excitement.

Unlike the intentionally fleeting encounters of libertine clubs, phone numbers and emails are regularly exchanged at fetish soirées, relationships are formed, and a certain level of trust established before the kinky games commence. That doesn't rule out casual sex among fetishists, *au contraire*. If the leather-clad hunk at the bar turns you on, there's nothing preventing you from reeling him in for a night of mutual enjoyment.

Who Goes?

Fetish parties bring together an incredibly diverse population of people of all ages, backgrounds, orientations and inclinations. You might encounter 20-something Goth clubbers covered in tattoos and piercings, a middle-aged dominatrix in a skin-tight rubber catsuit, a transvestite in a French maid outfit, a man with a dog collar following around his mistress on all fours, or a masked woman of uncertain age being spanked by a distinguished gentleman dressed as a military officer.

At the annual Nuit Dèmonia, a young Australian woman in her 30s is posing for the official event photographer. She's wearing a tightly-cinched red satin corset dress, a pair of sheer black seamed stockings and red retro platforms. She looks like she walked right off the cover of a vintage pin-up calendar. "I'm a huge fan of Dita von Teese," she admits, adjusting the elbow-length satin gloves. "This is my third year coming here. I just love dressing up…being someone totally different for a night." She winks at a man with a shaved head and a chain mail tunic, waiting patiently for his turn to be photographed. "These are the people your mother warned you about!" she says with a laugh. "But seriously, everyone is totally cool. Some of my friends think I'm crazy, but I think all women should try this at least once."

Sadomasochistic Literature

The term 'Sadism' comes from the French aristocrat Marquis de Sade (1740-1814), whose pornographic writings mirrored his own shockingly violent (and often non-consensual) sexual proclivities. His Austrian contemporary, the novelist Leopold von Sacher-Masoch (1836-1895), inspired the term 'Masochism' after romanticizing sexual servitude in his books such as Venus in Furs. One of the most scandalous sado-masochistic novels of the 20th century, The Story of O, was actually written by a woman, Pauline Réage, to impress her lover.

Your First Time

If you're new to the scene, you might get the impression you're walking into a den of Hell's Angels. But fear not, *Mesdames*; as scary as a dungeon full of torture instruments looks, no one will simply grab you, tie you up and commence with a caning – unless you ask. The main purpose of both the clubs and soirées is to dress up and socialize with like-minded people, so newcomers shouldn't feel obliged to participate in any sexual or sadomasochistic activities typically reserved for experienced practitioners and their partners. Of course, the small talk at these soirées may be somewhat different than what you're accustomed to, with lines such as: "So, are you dominant or submissive?" Unlike most libertine establishments, fetish clubs and soirées are generally open to couples, singles, or even groups of friends, as long as you're over 18 and properly dressed. "But this is not a zoo for gawking," explains one event organizer. "We welcome anyone genuinely interested in discovering the fetish lifestyle."

What to Wear

Dress codes depend on the soirée or club, but almost universally consist of at least one article of leather (*cuir*), PVC (*vinyl*), or latex clothing. Other dress code categories may include sexy uniforms, Goth, Japanese Manga, transvestite (for men), and "bizarre" science fiction or fantasy looks. As a rule, the bigger the soirée, the more elaborate the outfits. Of course, you could simply get away with a "civilian" look of a leather skirt with sexy top and heels, but dressing up is part of the fun. How often do you get the chance to wear a fire engine red latex dress or an Amazonian warrior costume? Browse the racks of the city's excellent fetish clothing boutiques for inspiration (see the **Get in the Mood** chapter for addresses).

Naughty Tip: If you don't arrive in your outfit, you can change inside and then leave your civilian clothes in the cloakroom. Space and privacy may be limited, so be savvy and wear something over your fetishwear that you can simply pull off when you arrive.

Fetish Etiquette

As in the libertine community, everyone is expected to observe the rule of mutual respect. An open mind and a sense of humor (*sans* inappropriate giggling) can diffuse any situations that might otherwise be potentially embarrassing or uncomfortable for newcomers. It's not uncommon for women to be approached by submissive men (usually on all fours) with specific requests such as: "May I kiss your shoes?" or "Will you whip me?" Don't be the wet blanket on someone else's fantasy by making a scene or otherwise losing your cool. If you're not keen on playing, a polite "*Non, merci*" will suffice.

If you would like to watch the BDSM activities taking place in the "dungeon," remain as silent and discreet as possible. Voyeurs are welcome, but you should make an effort to avoid interrupting or interfering with the scenes taking place, just as you would in a theatre. Photos are obviously a no-no unless you have the permission. And remember that no matter how disturbing, cruel or painful some acts may appear, these are simply very convincing performances between consenting adults living out their fantasies.

Like a Virgin...or Not!

According to the Kinsey Institute of Indiana University, 5-10% of Americans engage in light SM on at least an occasional basis. And if you've ever been blindfolded, tied up, or spanked by your lover during sex, you can count yourself among them.

Safety

There's no harm in a bit of whipping and bondage between consenting adults, right? But do be aware that there are certain precautions that need to be taken when playing these adult games. If you're an SM "virgin," it's not a good idea to simply pick up a bullwhip and start cracking away at your partner's exposed flesh. Contrary to appearances, the goal isn't actually to cause any physical harm. You'll have no trouble finding an experienced hand at these clubs willing to demonstrate the proper technique – someone to show you the ropes, as they say. If you've already perfected your flogging form, then by all means feel free to inspect the eligible submissives at your disposal. Likewise, make sure you clearly communicate your own limits to any potential playmates if you find yourself on the receiving end of a naughty spanking.

CRIS ET CHUCHOTEMENTS
9 RUE TRUFFAUT, 17TH
TEL 01 42 93 70 21
M° PLACE DE CLICHY
WWW.CRIS-ET-CHUCHOTEMENTS.COM

Yes, "Screams and Whispers"...and the sharp crack of whips, metallic clicks of handcuffs, low moans of pain...and pleasure. Follow the sounds into the vaulted stone dungeons of this exquisite Parisian fetish club. At the bottom of the stairs you'll find a surprisingly cozy candlelit lounge bar with period furnishings that the Marquis de Sade himself would surely appreciate. All very civilized, right down to the umbrella stand filled with riding crops of different shapes and sizes. A narrow passage next to the bar leads to a small flogging room equipped with a St-Andrew's Cross. Up the spiral staircase are more SM playrooms with human-sized cages, bondage pulleys, and a comfortable mattress nook. Very particular fantasies are reenacted in the old-fashioned study and tiled medical examination room. The mood is usually quite serious, even intense in the *salons*. An exception to this would be during the good-humored "Vente aux Esclaves" (Slave Auction, once monthly) and the Friday afternoon "Goûters du Divin Marquis" where your love slave can feed you fresh fruit and cakes as you watch fetish film screenings.

Hours & Rates

Tuesday to Saturday from 10:30 p.m. until dawn. Entry €49 (€69 for theme nights) for couples (one drink each included), €99 for single men (drink included), single ladies free. Extra drinks €13-€16. Friday afternoons from 3 p.m. – 9 p.m. "Les Goûters du Divin Marquis" €40 for couples, €45 for transvestites, €50 for single men, free for single ladies. Fruit and dessert buffet. Drinks €15.

Dress Code

Leather, latex, PVC, Pin-Up or Goth looks welcomed, but a very sexy black outfit is usually tolerated. In a pinch, your man can rent a black shirt or pants from the cloakroom.

Whenever a taboo is broken, something good
happens, something vitalizing. Taboos,
after all, are only hangovers, the product of
diseased minds, you might say, of fearsome
people who hadn't the courage to live and
who, under the guise or morality and reli-
gion, have imposed these things upon us.

—HENRY MILLER

NUIT DÈMONIA

LA LOCO
90 BOULEVARD DE CLICHY, 18TH.
Mº BLANCHE
WWW.NUITDEMONIA.COM

Coming to Paris in December? Don't miss the largest annual fetish soirée in France, sponsored by the Boutique Dèmonia, which takes place in a three-level nightclub next door to the Moulin Rouge. Approximately 2000 fetishists from every corner of the globe attend each year, including fetish models, photographers, artists, dominatrix, and BDSM performers. Those who arrive when the doors open at 8 p.m. can take advantage of the restaurant to dine "in character." There's a little bit of everything at the Nuit Dèmonia, including four bars for socializing, an official photo studio to capture your sexy ensemble for posterity, a foot massage booth, fetish art exhibitions, and a fully-equipped "couples only" dungeon. The huge dance floor on the main level becomes a stage for fetish fashion shows, bondage demonstrations and other kinky performances from 10 p.m. until midnight, followed by dancing until dawn to a different DJ every hour. Three other established Paris fetish soirées are organized the same weekend – La Nuit Elastique, Pervarty, and the Fetish Ciné-Club – with special passes available so that you can attend all four at a discount.

Dates & Rates

The annual Nuit Dèmonia takes place in early December. Entry is the same for everyone, whether you're a couple, man, woman, or transvestite. Tickets are sold well in advance at reduced rates (€20-€40), otherwise at the door for €50. Weekend Pass for the four parties (Nuit Dèmonia, Nuit Elastique, Pervarty, Fetish Ciné-Club), €60.

Dress Code

Everyone is required to wear a minimum of a skirt or pants in leather, latex or PVC in any color, including transvestites and those in fetish uniforms. The website has an excellent page with photos of what passes… and what doesn't.

LA NUIT ELASTIC

CAVES LECHAPELAIS
7 RUE LECHAPELAIS, 17TH.
TEL 06 62 34 57 10
M° LA FOURCHE
WWW.NUIT-ELASTIQUE.COM

Every month since 1998, approximately 300 aficionados gather at this club near Montmartre to dance and socialize in their finest fetishwear. Sometimes there's a back room dungeon for SM activities, but most of the mingling takes place at the bar and on the dance floor, where DJs play a mix of rock, new wave, electro, industrial and 80s music. This is not a libertine club or SM party, so there's a good balance of singles, couples, and groups of friends. "You don't have to be particularly rich, elegant or connected to take part in our soirées," explains the organizer, Francis Dedobbeleer. "Our evenings are for everyone… no need to be a superbimbo, an anorexic fetish model, or a male with the body of an athlete to have fun!"

Dates & Rates

The Nuit Elastique takes place every second Saturday of the month except in August. Happy Hour (10 p.m. –11 p.m.) entry is €5 for women and transvestites, €15 for men. From 11pm until dawn the price is €20 for everyone, or €15 if you pre-purchase your tickets at the Boutique Dèmonia (see the **Naughty Shopping** section).

Dress Code

The dress code is strictly enforced at these soirées, so as a minimum your pants or skirt should be leather, latex, or PVC.

FETISH IN PARIS

TEL 06 29 42 70 38
WWW.FETISHINPARIS.COM

This "Cozy Fetish Soirée" takes place in classy lounges throughout central Paris. Organized by the "French Fetish Association" founders Hugo and fetish wear designer Mademoiselle Ilo (www.mademoiselle-ilo.com), the emphasis at these convivial parties is on "extraordinary looks." Strut your sexy stuff on the dance floor, where the predominantly 30-something crowd dances to industrial, 80s, rock and techno DJ music. Video screenings, fetish fashion shows, free buffet, and a friendly welcome for an absolutely *charmante soirée*.

Dates & Rates

Parties take place monthly from 10:30 p.m. until dawn. Check the website for the exact date and location or stop by Métamorph'ose (see the **Naughty Shopping** chapter) for the latest flyer and advance ticket sales. Entrance €20 (€15 in advance), includes one drink and free buffet.

Dress Code

You can bet that everyone makes an extra effort to look fabulous at a party hosted by a fetishwear designer. The minimum requirements are a skirt or pants in latex, leather or PVC, but these materials aren't required if your outfit is truly *extraordinaire*. And no, nudity doesn't count as an "outfit."

LA PERVARTY
WWW.PERVARTY.COM

Even the most divinely deviant ladies might cringe at the unfortunate title of this soirée, but don't let the word *perv* fool you. Organized several times a year, this "Fetish Arty Party" is one of the more artistic evenings on the Parisian fetish circuit, where stage performances (including shibari, SM, and fetish fashions) take priority over back room or dungeon antics. Dress code PVC, latex, leather, transgender, pin-up, "over sexy," and uniforms.

ZINELLA'S FETISH & LIBERTINE SOIRÉES
WWW.ZINELLA.COM

Michael Zinella organizes regular fetish-SM-libertine parties in venues throughout Paris. Considered by some to be more hardcore, there is always a fully-equipped dungeon for those looking to engage in a little BDSM play. The atmosphere remains quite sociable at the bar and dance floor, where the regulars in this tight-knit community catch up. Newcomers and solo females welcomed. Dress code leather, PVC, latex, transvestite, uniforms and "bizarre."

Naughty Resources

Clubs come and go, parties change venues, and new events are created at any given moment. To keep up with the scene, check out the soirées calendar (*agenda*) on the **Dèmonia** (www.demonia.com) or **PsykoDollz** (www.psykodollz.com) websites. You can also pick up flyers advertising soirées and clubs at many of the boutiques listed in the "Naughty Shopping" section of the ***Get in the Mood*** chapter, including Phylea, Metamorph'Ose, Dèmonia, and La Musardine bookstore. Musardine also publishes an annual guide, *Paris Sexy* (in French only), a rather hardcore guide to all of the sex clubs, saunas, and gay cruising spots in and around the city.

It's a fantastic thing to take the risk of getting so close to your desires, expressing your obsession so absolutely. —JEANNE MOREAU.

Practical Information

Addresses

The city's 20 *arrondissements*, or districts, are designated as "1st" for *1st arrondissement*, "13th" for the *13th arrondissement*, etc. In a mailing address, the full zip code incorporates the *arrondissement* with the regional department code for Paris: 75. So *75001* would be in the 1st and *75013* in the 13th. Métro stations are abbreviated as "M°" when part of an address, so the *Métro Station St-Michel* becomes M° St-Michel.

Emergency Resources

Any neighborhood pharmacy can direct you to the nearest generalist doctor's office who accepts walk-ins (your hotel should be able to call for you, as well). A regular French doctor visit costs €21. Specialists (ie gynecologists) will often cost €50-€60. Many emergency and medical service workers in Paris speak basic English. Only go to the **American Hospital** (63 boulevard Victor Hugo, in the western suburb of Neuilly-sur-Seine, tel 01 46 41 25 25) as a last resort, since this private hospital will costs significantly more than its French counterparts. If you're not sure who to call, or just need someone to talk to, contact the English crisis line, **SOS Help** (phones open daily 3-11 p.m., tel 01 46 21 46 46).

Emergency Numbers
(free call from any phone)

Police 17
Medical Emergency 15
Fire and Paramedics 18
All emergency calls from cell phones 112

24-hours Doctor House Calls

SOS Médecins: tel 01 44 07 77 77
(the cost of a house call is €40-€75).

24-hour Pharmacies

Pharmacie Perrault: 6 place de Clichy, 9th, tel 01 48 74 65 18.
Pharmacie Les Champs Dhéry: 84 avenue des Champs-Élysées, 8th, tel 01 45 62 02 41.

International Planned Parenthood Federation

The French branch, *Mouvement Français pour le Planning Familial (MFPF)*, can supply the names of Paris hospitals and OB/GYN clinics: Tel 01 48 07 29 10. They have **two walk-in clinics**: 10 rue

Vivienne, 2nd (open Mon-Thur, tel 01 42 60 93 20) and 94 boulevard Masséna, 13th (open Friday, tel 01 45 84 28 25).

Essential Phrases

It's easy to score major brownie points with the Parisians with just a few simple phrases:

S'il vous plaît (see voo play') – **Please**
(This is the polite way to get attention in a café or restaurant, never "*Garçon!*")

Pardon/Excusez-moi — **Pardon/Excuse me.**

Whenever you visit a boutique, bakery, café, etc, you should always greet the owner/staff when you enter and say thank you and goodbye when you leave:

Bonjour/Bonsoir, Madame/Monsieur — **Hello/Good Evening, Madam/Sir.**
Merci, au revoir, Madame/Monsieur — **Thank you, goodbye, Madam/Sir.**

If you need assistance in a shop, always say hello first, then this phrase before your question:
*Excusez-moi de vous déranger, Madame/Monsieur (*Ex coo'

zay mwah' duh voo day' ron zhay', mad dam' mon syur') – **Excuse me for bothering you, Madam/Sir.**

Parlez-vous anglais? – **Do you speak English?**
(You should always ask this before starting to speak in English; never assume they can understand you.)

Tip: For more helpful vocabulary and pronunciations, see the **French Tongue** section of the **Get in the Mood** chapter.

Getting Around

Public transportation in Paris is inexpensive, efficient, and easy-to-navigate. In most cases it's the best way to quickly get around town. Every address in this guide has the nearest metro station listed (**M°**) for easy reference purposes, however ladies dressed up for a night out on the town should take a taxi instead. An average ride across town after dark is about €12. Reserve a **taxi** in advance by calling 01 45 30 30 30. The best way to get to and from the airport is to book a shuttle company such as **Airport Connection** (Tel 01 43 65 55 55, www.parishuttle.com).

Internet Access

If you bring your laptop to France, you'll need an adaptor plug (French outlets accept the rounded, two-prong plugs). Don't forget to contact your ISP in advance for the local dial-up number in France, otherwise you'll be billed for an international call. Most hotels and cafés now have WiFi, and in all municipal buildings and parks it's free. Internet cafés are still relatively easy to find in Paris. **Milk Internet Hall** (Tel 08 20 00 10 00; www.milklub.com) has seven locations in Paris open 24/7, the largest at Les Halles (31 boulevard de Sebastopol, 1st, M° Châtelet or Etienne Marcel).

Maps

Free fold-out maps are usually available at hotels and tourism offices, but these are hard to read, don't include every street, and brand you immediately as a tourist. Instead, invest in the small book *Paris par Arrondissement*, available for under €10 at any newsstand. As its title indicates, each arrondissement has its own page, with an index of streets and metro and train stations.

Money

The French currency is the Euro. Cash is always king, but a close runner up is the credit card (Visa and MasterCard are the most widely accepted; American Express is accepted in more upscale boutiques and restaurants). Exchanging cash or Travelers' Cheques is expensive and tedious. Order a small amount of Euros from your home bank to bring with you, then use your ATM card to withdraw more Euros once you arrive in Paris from any bank's cash distributor (you must know your 4-digit PIN).

Opening Hours

Larger shops are open Monday-Saturday 9:30 a.m. – 7 p.m. Smaller boutiques may be closed on Mondays, and the chain stores on the Champs-Elysées and other tourist-heavy areas remain open on Sundays. There are no 24-hour supermarkets in France, but many neighborhoods have small a late-night convenience store. The French use a 24 clock for telling time, so 9h00 = 9 a.m., and 21h00 = 9 p.m. ("h" stands for *heure*, or hour).

Safety

Paris is a relatively safe city, compared to many others in Europe, with a far lower rate of violent crime than in the US. Petty theft and purse snatching make up about 65% of all reported crimes. Keep an eye on your belongings at café terraces, crowded metros and major tourist sites such as Notre Dame, Champs Elysées, Sacré Cœur, Pompidou Center, Porte de Clignancourt flea market, and the Eiffel Tower. Women on their own should use common sense when out after dark. Stick to busy, well-lit streets and trust your instincts. After 10 p.m., avoid hassles by taking taxis instead of the metro, keeping away from Pigalle and Les Halles, and ignoring anyone (especially groups of young men) who try to talk to you on the street.

Smoking

Smoking is now banned in all indoor public spaces in France (including your hotel room), however café terraces are still fair game for nicotine addicts.

Tax & Tipping

Taxes are included in the price of any item sold in France. When spending more than €175 in one shop, be sure to ask the sales assistant if you're eligible for the Value Added Tax reimbursement (*TVA*, or *Détaxe* in French). Tipping in France is appreciated, but hardly required like it is in the United States, since the 15% service fee is included as part of your bill in restaurants, bars and cafés (even if it's not itemized on the receipt). If you feel you've received good service, feel free to leave a Euro in cafés, or tip 10% in more expensive restaurants (cash only; there is nowhere to add a tip to a credit card payment).

Telephones

Parisian phone numbers have ten digits starting with "01" (ie: 01 55 44 33 22). Cell phone numbers begin with "06" and special hotlines begin with "08". When dialing a French number from outside the country, replace the initial "0" with the French country code, "33" (ie: +331 55 44 33 22). To make international calls from France, dial "00" before the full number. For calling card or collect calls from France, contact the AT&T international operator (toll-free, in English): 0800 99 00 11. Public phones can only be used with pre-paid phone cards (*carte téléphonique*), approximately €10-€20 from any post office, news stand, or tourism office. To use your cell phone in Paris, be sure to find out in advance how to do this and what the rates will cost. Another option is to rent a cell phone in Paris from agencies such as **Context Paris** (Tel 01 72 81 36 35; www.contexttravel.com).

Toilets

The correct way to ask for the restroom in France is *"Les toilettes, s'il vous plaît?"* You may also see a sign pointing to "WC". Public toilets, now completely free, are often found near major monuments, inside metro stations, and parks. Keep some loose change in your pockets in case restrooms in cafés or brasseries are locked (you can also ask your server for a coin if you're a client).

Travel Resources
Paris Tourism Office

25 Rue des Pyramides, 1st,
M° Pyramides
Tel 08 92 68 30 00
www.parisinfo.com

Ile-de-France Regional Tourism Office

Carrousel du Louvre
99 Rue de Rivoli, 1st
M° Palais-Royal/Musée du Louvre
Tel 08 26 16 66 66 or 01 44 50 19 98
www.pidf.com_

France Guide

Maison de la France
www.franceguide.com
The official website of the French Government Tourist Office.

Secrets of Paris

www.secretsofparis.com
An online resource guide to Paris by Heather Stimmler-Hall.

Recommended Guidebooks

LUXE City Guides: Paris
www.luxecityguides.com

Time Out Paris: Eating & Drinking
www.timeout.com

Where to Wear Paris
www.wheretowear.com

Fodor's Paris Guide
www.fodors.com

Paris Eyewitness Travel Guide
www.dk.com

About the Author

Heather Stimmler-Hall had more fun researching this guidebook than she's willing to admit. She first came to Paris in 1995 with a background in news journalism and environmental policy. After a year as the Travel Editor for ELLE.com in 1999, she became a full-time freelance travel writer, specializing in guidebooks on Paris and the French Riviera. Today Heather writes about Paris in her website Secrets of Paris (www.secretsofparis.com) and leads private tours throughout the city. After receiving countless "discreet inquiries" into the naughtier side of Paris, she knew it was time to write this guide.

Author photo by Stephen Zezza

About the Photographer

Kirsten Loop and Heather met on the French Riviera in 2001, when Kirsten came to photograph "the light" and the open food markets for a year's break from Toronto's chilly winters. It wasn't hard to tempt her back to France once the theme of the guidebook was revealed. Heather was sure Kirsten could capture the female-empowering spirit she was looking for.

www.loopphotography.ca

Merci!

I'm eternally grateful for the enthusiasm and inspiration of Carolyn Heinze, a witty writer with a wicked grin who helped me develop the original concept of a naughty guide for good girls.

Naughty Paris wouldn't have been possible without the advice, assistance, and unwavering support from countless friends and colleagues along the way who doubled as research assistants, focus groups, copy editors, models for the photo shoot, and inadvertent therapists during my times of indecision, doubt and writer's block: Cassie & Mathew, Sylvia P., Karen S., Claire W., Coach Hathaway, Sophia K., Cynthia M., Ethan G., Jean T., Philippe V., Caroline M., Tony & Sage, Charmaine S., Tina & François, Laura K., Eric & Kath, Gary Lee K., Lord Brett, and all of the Secrets of Paris readers and tour clients who have been cheering me on.

Special thanks to Kirsten Loop for maintaining your sense of humor and sharp focus despite the sleep deprivation and less-than-ideal lighting conditions; to Stephen Clarke, Brian Spence, Terri Kempton and Connor Cochran for all of your encouragement and advice on the world of publishing; to Victoria Vesta and Leslie Seaton for your wise insights and constructive criticism; to Brenna Fleener, Lily Heise, Lisa Pasold and "Petite Brigitte" for the much-needed female camaraderie on research outings; to Jina Bacarr, Grace Teshima & Context Paris for spreading the word; and to the tireless Naughty Paris photo crew and models: Aarathi, Marcus, Eva, Amber, Maxim, Oonagh, Joann, Alexis, Bremner, and Monsieur Ullmann. Thanks also to Rebecca Friedman at Sterling Lord, photographer Ernesto Timor, designer Karen Vavra, and writers Allison Lightwine and Rebecca Catt for contributions made to this guide in its earliest stages.

Finally, much love and gratitude to my family for being such an important part of my life. This guide isn't for you, but I hope you'll come visit me in Paris anyway!

PHOTO CREDITS

All photos taken by Kirsten Loop
of Loop Photography except for the
following:

Courtesy Crazy Horse Cabaret, 143, 246
Courtesy Five Hotel, 60
Courtesy Flûte l'Etoile, 212
Courtesy Nuits Blanches, 172
Courtesy Pershing Hall, 219
Courtesy Salon Nouvelle Athènes, 98
Courtesy Salons Shiseido, 93
Courtesy Hotel Sezz, 58
Courtesy Stephen Zezza, 236
Author photo by Stephen Zezza, 289

Index